Praise for: *How to lift depression ...fast*

"Whether you yourself are depressed or you _____
friend, family member or client, this is an em_____
invaluable techniques and exercises for movin_____
And there is nothing complicated here – sugge_____ ___ ___ simple and
immediately useful ... Read, use, enjoy and reap the benefits for yourself
and others." *Ruth Morozzo, Footnotes Magazine*

"As a GP I see many people suffering from depression, and have searched
for years for a good book to recommend to them. At last I have found
one ... written in a style which makes the ideas easy to understand and
put into practice. I believe that the 'human givens' approach is a major
step forward in helping people suffering from depression and other
mental health problems." *Dr Gina Johnson*

"I can't recommend this book enough. I have spent a lot of money and
time researching my depression and I can say this is without doubt the best
book I have read on the subject. I urge you to buy it. I'm sure like myself
it will put you well on the road to recovery." *Reader Review, Amazon*

"An invaluable resource ... easy to read and understand ... offers much
practical help and advice." *Professional Social Work Journal*

"I recommend the book *How to lift depression ...fast*. Rather than spending
months and years exploring all the things that have gone wrong in your
life, human givens therapists provide you with the tools, insights and
support to turn your mood, focus and life around quickly."
Dr Mark Atkinson

"PLEASE, PLEASE read this book if you have depression or buy it for
yourself if someone close to you does. Depression is extremely nasty –
extremely disabling and amazingly powerful – and, to conquer it, you need
enabling and powerful information. I am evangelical about the advice and
theories provided by the 'human givens' approach and honestly believe
that reading this book can do only good for anyone wanting to escape
depression – and escape it for good. I hope the content of this book helps
you as much as it has helped me." *Reader Review, Amazon*

"Everyone involved in administering personal therapy should read this
book." *Nursing Standard*

"Really easy to read with fantastic tips and explanations. It only takes a
day to read this book even if you have trouble concentrating. A worth-
while investment for anyone who has, is caring for, or just has an interest
in treating, depression. The best self-help – a few easy adjustments to my
life and my sleep is much better and I wake up feeling refreshed (that's
in two weeks)." *Reader Review, Amazon*

The Human Givens Approach Series is a new range of books, each of which explores a recognised psychological or behavioural problem and shows in clear, non-jargonistic language how to treat it effectively with psychological interventions.

Other titles in the series include: *Freedom from Addiction: the secret behind successful addiction busting* and *How to Master Anxiety: All you need to know to overcome stress, panic attacks, phobias, trauma, obsessions and more.* Future titles will cover: anger, psychosis, disturbed children, self-harming, antisocial behaviour, workplace stress and saving families. (The series is part of a larger nationwide effort to move counselling, psychotherapy and education away from ideology and more into line with scientific findings about how the brain works and what people really need to live fulfilling lives.)

Joe Griffin is a research psychologist with graduate and postgraduate degrees from the LSE. He is hugely influential in the world of psychotherapy and is director of studies at the Human Givens Institute. He is co-author with Ivan Tyrrell of numerous titles including *Dreaming Reality: How dreaming keeps us sane or can drive us mad,* and, *Human Givens: A new approach to emotional health and clear thinking.*

Ivan Tyrrell is the Principal of MindFields College, the only specialist psychology college in the UK which educates over 12,500 professionals, including psychotherapists, counsellors, social workers, psychologists, nurses, doctors, psychiatrists, youth workers, occupational therapists, teachers, NHS and social welfare staff, each year on its courses.

Denise Winn is a journalist specialising in psychology and medicine, and editor of the *Human Givens* journal.

How to lift depression
[...*fast*]

Change is much easier than you think...

Joe Griffin & Ivan Tyrrell

with Denise Winn

How to lift depression

[...*fast*]

A practical handbook

PUBLISHING

Joe Griffin & Ivan Tyrrell

with Denise Winn

PUBLISHING

First published in Great Britain 2004
Reprinted:
2005 (twice), 2006, 2007

Published by HG Publishing, an imprint of Human Givens Publishing Ltd,
Chalvington, East Sussex, BN27 3TD, United Kingdom.
www.humangivens.com

A catalogue record for this book is available from the British Library.

ISBN 1-899398-41-4
ISBN-13 978-1-899398-41-6

Typeset in Book Antiqua and Conduit Condensed.
Printed and bound in Great Britain
by CPI Antony Rowe.

*Do not carry your year's
burden on one day.*

PROVERB

CONTENTS

Acknowledgements

We would like to thank Mike Beard, Pat Williams and Pamela Woodford for contributing some of the case histories for this book, and Jane Tyrrell for her many helpful suggestions and attention to detail.

The many reasons for hope

---

*I*F YOU are reading this book, it is likely you or someone you care about is suffering from depression. Or maybe you are interested because your work brings you into contact with people who are depressed and you want to know how to help them.

If it is you who are depressed, the fact that you are looking at this book is a good sign in itself, as it shows that you are motivated to get yourself better. If you are concerned about someone else, who seems too deeply depressed to want to do anything for themselves, then this book – although 'addressed' to the person with depression – will give you practical advice for helping them take the first crucial step towards recovery, and the many steps that will then follow on much more easily.

You may find this book startling and exciting because it could shake up a lot of ideas you had about depression and make you feel much more empowered to deal with it. For instance, people commonly don't realise that:

- depression is not a biological illness
- there is a simple explanation for the feelings of dire exhaustion, lack of motivation and tearfulness that accompany depression – and they can usually be easily shifted
- understanding what depression really is, is the first powerful step towards cure
- drugs are not the best treatment
- psychological approaches should not be painful – effective counselling should make you feel better immediately, not worse
- 75 per cent of people come out of depression with no help at all within six months, and much more quickly with the right kind of help.

We hope you will find this book uplifting and that it will help you to get out of depression (or help you bring others out of depression) faster than you would ever have imagined. Some people recover fastest with the assistance of a profess-ional, so we also provide information to enable you to recog-nise the kind of counsellors who will be effective as well as empathetic. This is so important. Counsellors may be nice, sympathetic and offer a listening ear, but that alone rarely cures depression. And those 'psychotherapists' who endlessly explore your past and psychoanalyse it are known to make depression worse. Through case histories, we show you how effective counsellors can work swiftly to help you lift depression and move on with your life.

We are not going to tell you to "cheer up" or to "snap out of it" or even to "look on the bright side". Before you can do anything to deal with depression, you need the correct knowledge and tools. Over the past 20 years, we have worked with hundreds of depressed people, young and old. We know that what cures depression isn't dwelling on it, "seeing it through" or digging deeper into it by looking for the 'whys' and 'wherefores'. What helps is getting the depressed person to stop worrying and get their basic physical and emotional needs met, stop brain exhaustion and rebuild their energy levels and self confidence. We call this the human givens approach to therapy.

How to help you apply it, for yourself or for others, is the aim of this book.

PART 1

Understanding depression

*I*T MAY have started gradually. You slowly become aware that you are feeling miserable most of the time. The world no longer seems so colourful and interesting. Perhaps you are still able to keep on working or doing your daily tasks, but you take less and less part in social activities and hardly see friends. Then the low-grade miserable feeling gets worse – broader and deeper. You can't keep your mind on what you are doing. At night, you can't get to sleep for the worries going round and round in your head, or you wake early and can't get back to sleep. Or maybe you find yourself sleeping all day – a thick, unrefreshing sleep that is just a means of not being awake, a means of shutting out the suffering. And whenever you wake, you still feel exhausted. You can't motivate yourself to do much. Maybe you can't remember what, if anything, you did half an hour ago. Crossing a room may feel like struggling through wet concrete at every step. Even simple tasks, like pouring cereal into a bowl or opening a tin of soup, may seem too huge to contemplate and reduce you to tears. Or maybe you find yourself unable to *stop* moving, restlessly pacing up and down in a state of agitation and despair.

Perhaps you can't eat. Or perhaps you keep eating. Making decisions about the simplest of things can feel overwhelmingly difficult, or else nothing seems important enough to decide upon anyway. The sense that anything is meaningful has drained away. Nothing seems funny or fun anymore. The depression may feel so heavy it is physical: a pressure on your ribs, a weight on your eyelids, an irritant on your skin. You have lost all your confidence and no longer trust that your talents or skills have any value. You feel useless.

You probably find it difficult to concentrate for long on anything – even reading a paper or watching television. Talking to anyone for more than a few minutes is too demanding, and you can't listen to their talk either. You feel as if you are looking at the world through fog and find yourself strangely untouched by the bad or sad things that happen to others. Or else you feel acutely sensitive, and every sad tale or tragedy you hear about seems to confirm or deepens your own despair.

You may even be experiencing fear that takes the form of panic attacks or of being unable to be alone, because you are frightened of the menacing power of your thoughts. The biggest fear is that this is never, ever going to end. The thought of suicide may well have crossed your mind, or you may have even attempted it.

If you are suffering from depression, or have done so in the past, some or all of these experiences will probably strike a chord with you, and no doubt you have others of your own to add. When you get that low, you may feel you are in the grip of a terrible, unfathomable illness that you are powerless to fight against. Even if you have experienced and overcome depression in the past, you may still feel powerless to prevent it swallowing you up again out of the blue. To you, it is a demon, a life sentence, an unavoidable curse.

In fact, it isn't. **The monstrous, life-destroying experience of depression _can_ be outwitted, banished, eliminated, torpedoed, totally annihilated – by you.**

The first step is to understand what depression _really_ is – and what it does to both the mind and the body to deceive you into believing that it is an overwhelming, terrible illness. Knowledge is power, and you can use the new knowledge in this book to empower yourself to beat depression. Some people find that, once they understand the insidious process by which depression works, they can prise open its stranglehold immediately. (Many people have told

> 66 The first step is to understand what depression _really_ is ... 99

us that this was the case for them.) Others need a little more help.

In this first section, we are going to explain what we know about depression. Some of it is new knowledge that many doctors, psychiatrists and psychotherapists don't yet know or, like you, are only just starting to find out about. Because it contains highly important, life-changing information, we suggest you read it when you can give it your proper attention. During every depression, there are hours or days when you feel better or more alive than at other times (even though you may not remember them afterwards, for reasons we will explain later). Use those better times to concentrate on this book and learn what you need to do to create positive, lasting change.

What we mean by depression

If you feel miserable and bad about yourself much of the time, are increasingly preoccupied with negative ideas about your life and the world, don't feel motivated to do the things you used to enjoy or were good at, find everything an effort and sleep poorly, you have a form of depression.

For some people, depression is driven by guilt ("If only I hadn't had that affair/that drink, my marriage wouldn't have broken down/I wouldn't have had my car accident and hit that boy"). For some, it is driven by anxiety, founded or unfounded ("What if I am one of the people at work who are made redundant?" "What if my children are knocked down on their way home from school?"). For others, it is driven by anger ("If the hospital had treated my father better, he wouldn't have died"). And some experience a combination of all three.

Doctors consider nine specific symptoms when they are making a diagnosis of depression. These are:

- depressed mood
- loss of pleasure or interest in usual activities
- disturbance of appetite
- sleep disturbance
- feeling agitated or lethargic
- loss of energy

- feelings of worthlessness or guilt
- difficulties in thinking
- recurrent thoughts of death or suicide.

If, from asking questions during a consultation, they conclude that someone has suffered from depressed mood or loss of pleasure or interest in their usual activities, along with at least four of the other symptoms, for at least two weeks, they diagnose 'major' depression. They will then probably prescribe antidepressants and/or refer the patient to a counsellor. (The counselling offered usually takes the form of 'listening therapy', in which people are encouraged to talk and uncover their own solutions – very difficult, or they would have done so already – or cognitive-behaviour therapy, in which people are helped to examine and correct faulty thinking. Despite its currently being doctors' flavour of the month, cognitive-behaviour therapy is a cumbersome approach and, like 'listening therapy', can't quickly help lift depression at all.)

Whether depression is what doctors term 'major' or 'minor' is, of course, of only academic importance. All depression is disabling to some degree, and the earlier you act to avert it the better. It really is something you can nip in the bud.

To help you do that, we now need to dispel some incorrect and dangerous beliefs.

Depression is NOT a biological illness

It is a myth that depression is primarily a biological illness or genetically inherited. (Indeed, despite all the millions of pounds spent on genetic research and gene mapping, no gene for depression has ever been found.) If you have been told you have an illness caused by a chemical imbalance in your brain that you can't help, you may find what we are saying a bit shocking. In fact, it is actually the most empowering thing you could learn. It means *you* can be in charge of your recovery.

Unfortunately, despite all the scientific evidence to the contrary, a high proportion of psychiatrists and general practitioners still believe that depression is a biological illness and that it needs treating with the right drugs – and so that is the approach they take with their patients. But this belief doesn't make any sense when we look at the evidence.

- The amount of depression suffered is rising dramatically in the western world *all the time*, with the biggest increase being in young people and young adults. Thirty years ago, depression in young children was rarely reported. (If you are interested in statistics, take a look at the box on page 12).

- In thriving traditional societies, often called 'primitive societies', depression is minimal. However, when these

Recognising depression in others

IF YOU are concerned about the mental health of someone else, there may be other signs you should also be alert to. For instance, some people may seem downcast but complain of back pain, insomnia or migraine rather than depression. In young children, depression may take the form of apathy or terror of being apart from a parent, often expressed in clinging behaviour, unwillingness to go to school or recurrent fears that they or their parents are going to die.

All adolescents experience turbulent emotions as part of the growing up process but excessive negativity, irritability, sulking, complaints of not being understood, withdrawal from activities with family or friends and, sometimes, antisocial behaviour, can all be signs of depression. Increasingly, cannabis use is being linked with depression and behavioural problems in teenagers. Even just occasional use of ecstasy can significantly increase depression in some.

In elderly people, apathy may be the most obvious sign of depression and, importantly, memory loss and mild disorientation. The latter may sometimes be misunderstood as signs of dementia (or commonly accompany dementia, making the condition appear more advanced than it is). Understandably, fear of dementia can itself worsen anxiety and depression, and mimic its symptoms.

Often depression is not experienced on its own. People may have what doctors term 'co-morbid disorders' – another physical or psychological disorder that they are suffering at the same time. For instance, 60 per cent of people with ▶

societies become more westernised, their rates of depression start to increase rapidly.

● Research evidence shows that the vast majority of depressions lift, if treated by effective psychological methods, and that people helped by these methods relapse far less than people given drug treatments.[1]

The fact that depression has increased so strikingly in modern times, affecting different people of different ages and in different cultures at different rates, tells us something crucial about the nature of depression. Genes just don't change that fast. What *has* changed is our society. It is the changing nature of our lives and the way we live them that now leaves so many of us struggling to cope, and so susceptible to depression.

depression suffer simultaneously with anxiety disorders (anxiety is pretty much part and parcel of depression, as you will see). These anxiety disorders may range from severe, generalised anxiety to full-blown panic attacks. Other people may develop obsessive compulsive disorders or addictions – it is common for people who are depressed to turn to drink or drugs in an effort either to lift their mood or to blot out their misery. Sometimes it is the presence of a chronic physical disorder, such as back pain, multiple sclerosis or Parkinson's disease, that leads a person to become depressed. They then have to contend with both the illness and the depression.

While many of the advances of our modern, technological culture are to our benefit, the downside is that they often have consequences that go against human nature. Human nature is programmed into us from our genes and we experience it as the physical and emotional needs that have to be met in the world if we are to live healthy and fulfilled lives. More and more circumstances of modern life prevent us meeting our fundamental needs.

See if you can recognise, below, some circumstances that may apply to you.

Lack of support

Telephones, mobile phones, email, the internet: all keep us in touch – but increasingly keep us physically apart. We can cross the world at a speed that would leave our ancestors

---

Sometimes depression is triggered by medication

IT IS well established that some drugs used to treat certain physical conditions such as heart problems, high cholesterol, epilepsy or migraine, can cause depression in some people. However, there are many drugs that can be used to treat these conditions and changing to a different medication that suits you better should help the depression to lift. See your doctor if you think your depression could be caused, or worsened, by any medication you are taking.

gasping in disbelief yet, with that mobility and extra freedom, comes loss of community. It is all too easy to end up living far away from family and friends, often alone or as single parents. Community ties that once kept everyone looking out for each other (and that persist in traditional or small island societies) have weakened. In such circumstances, becoming ill, being made redundant or losing a loved partner can hit us all the harder.

Consumerism

An incredible range of material goods is available to us now, and the continual advertising that attracts us to them, coupled with the purchasing power to buy, entices us to confuse 'wants' with 'needs'. It is now considered normal to encourage greed in this way. Politicians sanctify it by calling it 'choice', as if this were inherently a good thing. (Even mentally healthy people can feel temporarily overwhelmed and depressed when shopping because of the range of similar products on offer. This comes about because of the nagging feeling that you can never know for sure if you are making the *right* choice!) The problem is that any society that has a preoccupation with 'choosing' and 'having' increases the self-absorption of its members. Self-absorption always becomes more pronounced in depression. (Often, it is only when people experience a serious illness, such as cancer, or suffer the unexpected loss of a close loved one, that they suddenly question their material life values for the

The rise and rise of depression

■ Of all the psychological disorders affecting people in the Western world, depression is the most common.[2]

■ In the UK alone, it is expected that half of all women and a quarter of all men will suffer depression at some point in their lives.[3]

■ In the four years between 1994 and 1998, the numbers of people seeking help from their GPs for depression soared from four million to nine million (although some of this rise might be accounted for by an increasing willingness to seek help).[4]

■ In the year 2000, 14 per cent of 42-year-old men and 21 per cent of 42-year-old women were depressed, compared with nearly half that number when they were nine years younger. Even more alarmingly, people who were 30 in the year 2000 were already as depressed as the 42-year-olds.[5]

■ Depression is rising in people of every age.[6]

■ The most rapid increase is in young people, aged between 15 and 25.[6]

■ There are also steep rises in the numbers of young people killing themselves, although rates of suicide, too, are increasing across all age groups, and in every country in the world.[7]

■ The World Health Organisation estimates that depression will be second only to heart disease as the leading cause of illness and death by 2020.[8]

first time. They may then adjust their outlook and make positive changes and search for more meaning and purpose from their activities.)

Relationships

We place far less emphasis nowadays on keeping the family intact. Couples have higher, more selfish, expectations of fulfilment in their relationships today and are inclined to separate rather than stay together 'to make it work' or 'stick it out for the children's sake'. In general, more priority is given now to the self and to personal aspirations than to social responsibilities – yet doing things for others has actually been shown to enhance mental and physical health.

Time pressure

New technology, in opening up opportunities, has created new pressures, too. We can work, shop and be entertained at all hours of the day and night so we struggle to pack more and more into every 24 hours. But our bodies and brains are designed to take regular breaks and, if we ignore that biological need, our stress hormones go into overdrive to keep us alert. The price we pay in the long term for keeping our stress levels so unnaturally high is eventual physical and emotional ill health. Another major casualty of our rush-rush society is we spend less time with the family.

Relaxation

Many people are so over-stimulated that they find it impossible to relax naturally without the aid of drugs and alcohol, TV or music. However, watching too much TV is actually exhausting and depressing in its own right, for reasons that will become clear later in this section.

Increasing uncertainty

Today people cannot leave their homes unlocked and many live in continual dread of crime and antisocial behaviour. We can no longer take it for granted that a job is for life, or that there will be a pension to retire on, or that the with-profits endowment policy will pay off the mortgage. And uncertainties about the state of the planet, global warming, terrorism, future wars and economic collapse, voiced by numerous prophets of doom, assail us from all sides and add to our worries.

No one, of course, can ever know for certain what lies ahead; that's always been true, but we have to plan our lives as if we do – because having a sense of control over our lives is essential for human health and happiness. Yet we also have to be ready to rise to the challenge of inevitable changes when they occur. In the current climate, you may feel as if your control over how you live and work is slipping away, and that can have serious repercussions in terms of mental and physical health, making you less able to deal positively with the unexpected.

The role of serotonin

Although the previous points are compelling social and psychological explanations for the rise in depression, which fly in the face of the belief that depression is a biological illness, we do not dispute for one minute that there is a biological *element* to depression. Every thought and every emotion that we experience changes our brain chemistry. The levels of the feel-good brain chemical serotonin fluctuate constantly, according to what we are doing and how we are feeling about ourselves. If we are depressed, we have low levels of serotonin, whereas, when we are feeling positive and acting positively, serotonin levels are high.

Although drug companies keenly promote the idea that depression arises from a chemical imbalance in the brain, it is now clear that the lowered serotonin levels found in the brains of depressed people are a *consequence* of depression, not a cause of it. This is affirmed by the fact we mentioned earlier – that the right kind of psychological treatment can help lift depression more effectively than antidepressants can. (More of that later.) Also, in 75 per cent of cases, depression just gets better on its own, within six months. That means that the all-important question to ask is this one:

"What is it that people start doing differently, with or without help, that makes the depression go away?"

It is a myth that difficult life situations cause depression

We have outlined some of the ways that modern life may put us at greater risk of depression. However, throughout the ages people have struggled with life threatening circumstances – war, famine, floods and disease – and survived great hardships without becoming depressed. It is not seemingly insurmountable difficulties, therefore, that cause depression.

Humankind is a remarkably adaptable species, or we would not have evolved as far as we have already. It is well known, for instance, that people who have survived even terrible torture or devastating sexual or physical abuse have, despite this, gone on to live happy, successful, mentally healthy lives. Very many parents have tragically lost a child to an illness, accident or suicide (surely one of the most emotionally painful experiences a human can undergo) yet have managed, after a natural period of grieving, to pick up their lives again. And, although the statistics show quite clearly that children from broken homes, on average, do less well emotionally and academically than children from intact, happy homes, a good proportion of the former do, in reality, excel.

The message is clear. *It is not circumstances that lead to depression but how you respond to them that matters.*

This can explain two other misconceptions.

MISCONCEPTION 1: Depression is an illness that you can get again and again

It isn't depression that is recurrent but the difficulties that life throws at us. It is because people tend to react to difficult circumstances with the same sort of attitude and responses each time that many people suffer from recurrent bouts of depression.

MISCONCEPTION 2: Depression is passed down, in the genes, through families

When we are children, it is our parents' responses and attitudes to circumstances that we are most intensely exposed to, and this is why we may seem to 'inherit' a tendency towards depression. But it isn't anything primarily genetic. It is mainly a learned response.

At its heart, depression arises because of some kind of loss: loss of loved ones through death or the ending of a relationship; loss of a job; loss of status; loss of friends and familiar activities, perhaps as a result of a house move to a different area; loss of looks; loss of health; loss of physical prowess or childbearing ability; loss of memory; loss of enjoyment; loss of purpose in life, and so on.

But it is part of the human condition to handle losses as we move through life. We must all face the fading of our looks, the stiffening of our limbs, the increasing forgetfulness, the death of older members of the family, and most of us manage these rites of passage successfully, if with some sadness. Of course, it is natural, at times, to feel temporarily overwhelmed by grief or by highly stressful events, but we then need to get back on our feet again. Research has shown that, even after suffering a serious physical disability, it is possible for people to regain their former levels of happiness, albeit doing different things. Even four out of five patients with healthy minds 'locked in' to paralysed bodies still rate their quality of life as good or satisfying, if they can communicate by some means. Human resilience is awe-inspiring.

Depression is always an unnecessary, additional, problem

Depression, as we know, doesn't change anything or make anything better. It is a signal that something is deeply wrong and, as with a signal of acute physical pain, it needs to be acted on at once. If depression is allowed to deepen and persist, all that happens is that you have the misery of depression to cope with, *on top of* whatever loss or difficulty was the initial trigger. The beloved partner is still dead; the important examination remains failed; the job redundancy is no less real.

But, instead of coming to terms with the difficult circumstances and dealing with the implications, the sufferer flounders helplessly, mired in a depression that seems to have a crushing will of its own.

So what is it that makes some people able to handle life's setbacks and sadnesses, whatever they are – face them and then move on – while others sink into depression?

Depression is a strong emotion

There are some distinct tendencies that distinguish the people who get depressed from the people who don't. If you recognise these tendencies in yourself, this will give you a powerful tool to work with, to help you make the changes that will lead you away from depression.

Black-and-white thinking

People in the grip of depression tend to think in either/or, black-or-white, all-or-nothing terms. For instance, someone who is depressed might wake up late and think, "I've overslept; I can't go to work," instead of ringing to say they will be delayed or recasting the day's plans in some way to ensure the necessary work gets done. If a colleague passes in the corridor without smiling, the depressive person is likely to think, "He didn't smile at me! He doesn't like me anymore," instead of considering that the person might have been preoccupied in thought, fully engaged in conversation with someone else or not feeling in a good mood himself. If a partner offers a suggestion for making the doing of some task a little easier, the depressed person interprets it as a criticism and says something like, "Well, do it yourself, then!" If one thing goes wrong, the whole day will be a complete write-off as far as a person who is depressed is concerned; they will discount or even forget all the things that went right.

This type of thinking is emotional thinking, not rational thinking, which isn't surprising, because it is done by the emotional brain. People often don't realise that depression is an emotion, a *strong* emotion. As you will be well aware yourself, even though you might look lifeless or listless to others when you are depressed, all sorts of highly charged feelings are churning around. Indeed, we know that, when people are depressed, their levels of the stress hormone cortisol soar! [9]

Emotions are generated from a part of the brain that is ancient in evolutionary terms. Our brains have evolved in stages over millions of years and the structures of the brain that are concerned with our emotions developed from the brainstem, the simplest, earliest part of the brain, which sits at the top of the spinal cord and regulates functions such as breathing and metabolism. This is equivalent to the brain of reptiles. When warm-blooded mammals evolved, our basic emotional repertoire gradually developed, to aid our survival in the wild. For instance, the experience of fear gets the body physically geared up for 'fight or flight' in the face of danger; anger makes it easier to attack whatever threatens us. Similarly, loving feelings in humans ensure a male will look after its mate and they will both look after their young.

Strong emotions focus and lock our attention. In survival terms, everything is simplified to a black or white choice: "Is this substance dangerous or is it safe? "Can I eat this or will it eat me?" "Should I fight or run away?" It was many million more years before the thinking part of our brain (the neo-cortex) developed out of the brain structures concerned with emotions. In other words, we were emotional long before we were rational. Once we evolved the ability to imagine, think, plan, evaluate, analyse, judge, etc, we became able to unlock our attention and respond, not just in an all-or-nothing, black-and-white way like an animal, but with a palette of the thou-

> 66 Strong emotions focus and lock our attention ... every-thing is simplified to a black or white choice ... 99

sands of possibilities in between. This means that, if we are startled by a sudden rustling in the bushes and see a black shape, the emotional brain still reacts first, prepared to set in motion the 'fight or flight' response if necessary. But, an instant later, the rational brain steps in to calm things down, by recognising the rustling object as an empty black plastic bag being blown about by the wind – no threat at all.

Thus, our judgements are formed by two types of intelligence: emotional and rational. Most of the time, they can work effectively in partnership together, with the rational brain adding subtlety and perspective to the emotional brain's raw feelings, and the emotional brain tempering the rational brain's clinical judgements. But emotions came first, as we said, and they still predominate, because of the survival link (even though it is rare these days for us to face rampaging animals). So, when feelings are very strong, they automatically overwhelm rational intelligence and prevent more subtle or wider viewpoints from being considered.

> 66 We have two types of intelligence: emotional and rational. 99

We all know from our own experience when we are in the grip of strong emotions, be it anger, fear, greed or new love, that our judgement becomes perilously clouded. We are in the right, we angrily insist, furiously refusing to hear any other argument. When greedy, we are easily conned into buying something we don't need. And the new beloved is perfect in every way – a view we can't believe we held when reality kicks in later and the scales fall from our eyes. In fact, when highly emotionally aroused, we often become downright stupid. The bigger picture disappears completely. It is no different with the strong emotion of depression. When the emotional brain is switched on full, the rational brain is switched to low. That is why depressed people can find themselves in a supermarket, completely incapable of deciding which soap powder they should buy.

Once the emotional brain takes over, it applies its primitive black-and-white, all-or-nothing, survival-type thinking. Either this is the case or that is the case. There is no in-between any more, no 'maybe', no 'perhaps it is because...' Everything is either good or bad, right or wrong, perfect or completely useless.

Whenever we are emotionally overwhelmed by events, we all tend to think this way for a while, but people who are not normally black-and-white thinkers snap out of it quite quickly. Some people, however, without realising they are doing so, tend towards this all-or-nothing thinking most of the time, and they are the ones more likely to sink into depression.

Personal, pervasive and permanent

How do you know if you are a black-and-white thinker? And what can you do about it?

The tendency is revealed most clearly in the ways we explain to ourselves the adverse events that happen in our lives. We all need to make sense of what happens to us. Psychologists have found that the way we do this has considerable bearing on whether we are more or less likely than others to develop depression.[10] What counts is how *personally* we take events, and how *pervasive* and *permanent* we think the effects will be.

As with everything, the more we understand something, the more we can protect ourselves from its ill-effects, so think about the following scenarios and decide whether the responses described are the type that you would be likely to make in such circumstances, particularly when you are in the grip of depression.

EXERCISE:

How personally do you take events?

- If the dinner didn't taste good and you were the cook, would you tend automatically to think it was your fault? Would you fail to think about whether the meal stayed in the oven too long because the people you were cooking for arrived late to eat it? Or whether the recipe instructions were unclear? Perhaps you added a little too much salt. Would you worry about it for some time afterwards, berating yourself for spoiling the occasion, rather than just apologising, shrugging it off and forgetting about it?

- If a relationship didn't work out or petered out quickly, would you tend to think you were the one to blame? Perhaps you should have been more affectionate or perhaps you were *too* affectionate, not allowing the other person sufficient space? Or perhaps you just weren't a lovable enough person? Or would you agonise about what it was that you clearly must have done wrong, to lose the love or interest of your partner? Would you think little or nothing about what habits or attitudes on your partner's side contributed to the breakdown of the relationship? Would you consider at all whether the pair of you weren't in fact a good match because of being incompatible – having different interests, attitudes to life and so on?

- If you had a boss who told you that your team was not performing as well as it should, would you instantly think that it was your own inadequate work that had let the team down, or worry that it might have been? Even if someone else on the team were patently slacking, would you expect the boss to think the culprit was you?

- If you worked at a company that closed down, causing you to lose your job, might you blame yourself for choosing that company, of all companies, to work for?

How pervasive do you think events will be?

- If your marriage or a romantic relationship ended, would you think that your whole life was ruined? Would the job you enjoy suddenly become meaningless? Would you struggle to be interested in your children's achievements at school?

- If you lost your job or failed to get offered one that you really wanted, would you tend to lose heart in everything? Might you see your whole life as a failure and respond negatively to suggestions from others that you should start looking in pastures new?

- If you were to suffer a serious disability, such as the loss of a limb or your sight, would you think about all the things you could no longer do? Would you assume that life could never be good or meaningful again?

How permanent do you think effects will be?

- After losing a job or failing to get offered one, would you think, "I'll *never* find another one!"?

- If a relationship ended or a loved partner died, would you think, "There will never ever be another person in the world whom I could love or who could love me"?

- If you had your heart set on buying a certain house but someone else's offer is accepted, would you imagine that you couldn't ever be happy again?

- If you failed an important exam, would you view your entire life as blighted?

Think of some of the setbacks or sorrows that are making you miserable in your own life now and ask yourself the same sort of questions as to how you are responding to them.

When people take most things personally and interpret events as having a far bigger or longer lasting impact than is really the case, they are exacerbating the black-and-white thinking style of the emotional brain by generating more and more emotion. In effect, they keep turning on the 'fight or flight' response. This gets them worked up into a stew of resentment and hostility, or a state of pure anxiety and consequent low self-esteem, and thinking in ever-more 'all-or-nothing' terms. If something doesn't go to plan or a relationship isn't perfect in almost every way, then it is a complete disaster. This is why so many people who are prone to depression also tend to be perfectionists. Everything has to be absolutely right; otherwise it is completely wrong. (Maybe you have noticed this about yourself!) The same tendency can also sometimes lead to excessive jealousy. This over-simplified, emotional thinking style also explains why, in the deep grip of depression, people can end up slumped on the floor, in floods of tears at the thought of the effort required to do something as simple as finding the can-opener to open a tin.

Depression makes us selfish

Try thinking of it this way. On the beach by the ocean we can hold a pebble close enough to our eyes to blot out all sight of the sea. But that doesn't mean that the sea isn't there. Similarly, when we focus on the negatives and let them loom large, they take on a power that isn't real and block out all the good things about life. It is the perspective we choose to take that makes up our world and determines the course our life takes in it, not the pebble in your hand nor the negative events that occur.

To put it bluntly, depression makes a person almost completely selfish. You are thinking all the time about how things affect *you* and how *you* feel about them. Tragedies in the world make *you* feel more miserable. *Your* life is ruined. You can't think about the needs or feelings of people – even those who love you – except

> " When we focus on the negatives and let them loom large, they take on a power that isn't real ... "

to feel bad about *yourself* for not thinking of them. Everything revolves around *you*. This is what the emotional thinking style of depression does to you. And it is the innate selfishness of depression that is hard for friends and family to tolerate. It can, if it goes on too long, even drive people away from you.

The powerful pull of pessimism

Clearly, as life rarely goes according to plan and no relationship is perfect, people prone to depression tend to be pessimistic about life and expect little of themselves or other people. Like the Sirens' song, this point of view is seductive. It lets the pessimistic person off the hook of having to make an effort to engage with the world and other people. They only have to consider a small number of possibilities: the negative ones. They cynically focus on a one-size-fits-all approach to life, the difficulties and downsides, and always decide not to embark on anything that could result in failure or disappointment, thus cutting down their chances of experiencing life to the full, with all its rewards and challenges. (Sometimes, of course, a pessimist is an optimist with extra information. If you know a business venture is being undertaken by incompetent people, you could be justified in holding a pessimistic view about the outcome.)

One serious outcome of a deeply pessimistic approach is that depressed people may not even think it is worth seeking help for themselves – because they are convinced that nothing could possibly work. If you are reading this book because you are depressed, take heart that you are already on the road to recovery. You clearly want to get better and find the ways to do so. If you are reading this book because you are the relative or friend of someone who is depressed, a pessimistic mindset is what you will be aiming to help them overcome. They have to learn to say "YES!" to opportunities that arise (as long as they are legal!).

Things happen

People who aren't depressive thinkers know that there are many possible causes for the things that happen in life. They don't automatically jump to the conclusion that they themselves carry the sole blame for any personal setbacks. They know that disappointment or loss affects only a small aspect of their lives and that, in time, they will surmount it.

People who are not prone to depression know this vital fact: life isn't *either/or*; it is *both/and*. Ask yourself the following questions:

- Can my partner make a stupid decision and still be intelligent?
- Can I say hurtful things to my children and still love them?
- Can my children respect me and still push at the boundaries I set?
- Can I love someone despite their faults?
- Can I be uncertain about my abilities and take on challenges?

A depressed person is more likely to answer 'no' to questions like these. Challenging an either/or mindset is an important task in the process of getting rid of depression, and we will be giving you plenty of practical guidelines for how to do so, in the second part of this book.

Depression is a signal that a person's needs aren't being met

Underlying the experience of depression is the fact that people who succumb to it are not having their needs met. If you were having all your needs met and your life were going swimmingly, you wouldn't be unhappily worrying about so many things! Depression is *always* secondary to another problem.

Every organism, from the simplest single-celled creature to a flowering plant or a human being, has needs which have to be fulfilled if it is to thrive. Human needs are much more complex than those of plants, of course. We will be looking at these in more detail in the second part of this book, because this is at the heart of the human givens approach. It is sufficient here to say that, to live an emotionally healthy life, we must be meeting needs such as those for intimacy, wider social connection, having a sense of autonomy or control over our lives and for feeling that our lives have meaning and purpose – however we interpret that. Failure to have such needs met, perhaps because we don't know how to or lack the necessary skills, can quickly spiral us down into depression.

Sometimes it is the fallout from a traumatic experience in the past that prevents needs being met. For instance, an experience of being bullied and beaten by one's peers at school may make someone reluctant to trust others later in life and therefore miss out on vital social connections with people. Over time, this is likely to result in depression because it is a human given that we should connect well to other people and we worry when we are not. (And it is worry that causes depression.) In such cases, resolving the traumatic memory, which can be simply done (as we show in the third part of this book) is often sufficient to resolve the depression.

> 66 Depression is *always* secondary to another problem. 99

Why depression is so exhausting

Depressed people often say, "Why am I so exhausted all the time?" It doesn't make sense, does it, when they are hardly getting out of bed or leaving the house at all? Surely they barely use up any energy slumped in a chair in front of the TV? For a long time there was no satisfactory answer a doctor or psychotherapist could give them. Yet it *is* a fundamental question and now we have the answer to it. And, when depressed people hear our explanation about the cycle of depression, it comes as a great relief. Indeed, the explanation itself is therapeutic. It is as if a light switches on for them. They can see for the first time why they are locked into exhaustion and depressive thinking, and what they need to do to get out of it. This is new psychological knowledge derived from the human givens approach.

Crucial to this is an understanding of REM sleep and the function of dreams.

REM sleep and depression

Most of our dreaming occurs in the stage of sleep that is known as rapid eye movement (REM) sleep, because in that state of brain activity our eyes dart about underneath our closed eyelids. When, many years ago, some people who were depressed were asked to take part in research in sleep laboratories, it was found that, if they were woken up every time they went into REM sleep, the next morning their mood had lifted. This happened even when the depression was severe. But the effects didn't last. Once people started to sleep uninterrupted again, the depression returned and very often became worse, because they had even more REM sleep than usual, to make up for the shortfall. At the time, no one understood why any of this should happen, but it definitely seemed that REM sleep had some connection with depression.

Electroconvulsive therapy (ECT), an often successful, if somewhat crude, treatment for severe depression, also has an impact on REM sleep. ECT was the most common treatment for depression before the development of antidepressant drugs. In olden times electric eels were applied to the head to achieve the same result. Today electrical currents are passed through the brain via electrodes applied to the temples. This induces seizures (convulsions). Doctors now give muscle relaxant drugs just before treatment to minimise the danger to the body caused by convulsions. Unfortunately (because ECT can cause severe memory loss) it is growing in popularity again, in a slightly more modernised form. The change in REM sleep that ECT causes results from the effects on the brain of the induced convulsions.

No one ever knew why exactly this treatment should halt depression or what the REM sleep connection with depression meant (antidepressant drugs also inhibit REM sleep) until one of the authors of this book, Joe Griffin, carried out his groundbreaking research into why we evolved to dream and the function of dreams. As a result, he formed what is now known as the *expectation fulfilment theory of dreaming*, which explains all of the features of depression. It is the only theory to do so.

Dreams deactivate unexpressed emotional arousal

Joe's research has shown that we dream at night to deactivate the emotional stuff we get worked up about during the day that is still taking up space in our brains when we go to sleep. However, we don't dream about *all* the emotionally arousing experiences that we have. We don't dream about the blazing row we had with our partner or our boss, nor do we dream about the enjoyable party we have just returned from. We only dream about events and thoughts that we *haven't* acted on or expressed in some way. In other words, we dream about emotionally arousing expectations which, unconsciously, our emotional brain is still anticipating. (Hence the 'expectation fulfilment' theory of dreaming.) For instance, suppose we pass a cake shop in the morning and experience a strong desire for some profiteroles. We push the desire aside because we are trying to eat healthily or because it is nearly lunchtime. However, although we then forget about the profiteroles, that awakened emotional impulse to eat them remains in our nervous system, waiting to be fulfilled. Similarly, if we are looking forward to going to a party or a concert on a particular night but we learn in the afternoon that we can no longer go, the expectation of the pleasure that we were going to experience still remains active in our nervous system.

In our conscious, rational minds, of course, we have made our decision not to eat some profiteroles or experienced our disappointment over the concert and moved on. We are not usually conscious that such expectations are still 'live' in our brains because they occur at an instinctive, emotional level. But, once a primitive urge is aroused – be it for food, sex or some other pleasure, or to defend oneself or escape from danger – it has to be discharged somehow. If it were not discharged, and the instincts were repeatedly being inhibited, then the underlying neural pathways would be rewired and we would cease to be able to spontaneously access those instincts. We need to keep our instinctive responses intact, so that they are available to us when we need them. (It is no good looking at a tree beginning to fall down right on top of us, and not having a strong urge to run.) So all expectations must be acted out somewhere, and nature adapted the REM state to be like an internal theatre where we could harmlessly fulfil our expectations in metaphorical form, thus de-arousing us. (This is explained more fully in our book *Dreaming Reality: why dreaming keeps us sane, or can drive us mad.*[11])

The unfulfilled expectations that give rise to dreams can be amazingly mundane. For instance, just watching a thriller on the television may arouse a fear response, or watching a sequence in a soap opera may arouse anxiety or anger, as we empathise with the characters. If we carry on thinking about it or being affected by it, the arousal is not discharged in waking life and so has to be discharged in a dream. This theory has been confirmed thousands of times, not just through Joe's research on his own dreams and those of others, but countless times since by people who have understood this insight and seen the process at work in their own lives.

Why depressed people dream more than is good for them

What is the especial relevance of this to depression? It quickly becomes clear. People who are depressed worry and ruminate constantly. They dwell on anxious, angry or guilty thoughts that make them miserable and keep them emotionally aroused. They worry in black-and-white terms about all the kinds of concerns we discussed earlier. "How am I going to cope with giving a dinner party when I am so inadequate in everything I do?" "What will I do if my partner of 15 years, who has been slightly grumpy lately, decides he or she wants to leave me?" "Why do I feel so miserable all the time?" "I'm such an awful person, because I'm making everyone else miserable as well. Do they hate me?" And so on, and so on. We all have a thought 'commentary' running in our heads and most of the time we aren't even conscious of the content of the thoughts. But, in the case of depressed people, the commentary is almost always negative. "I always make a mess of things." "He isn't going to think highly of me." "There's no future in this." "The whole world is in a terrible state, so what's the point of bothering to go on?"

Not much of this kind of emotional arousal gets discharged in the normal course of the day. Unlike anxiety about an exam that is about to be taken or a speech to be given, which is dispelled immediately the event is over, most of what concerns a depressed person is ill-defined. Worries, which arise from some aspect of physical or emotional needs not being met, tend to be about nebulous threatening possibilities. Or a depressed person may spend much time brooding over something that happened, or didn't happen, that cannot now be changed, or dwelling helplessly on current difficulties that seem too daunting to resolve. In other words, people who continually worry and brood are raising a lot of confused expectations but not doing anything to unravel or fulfil them. The negative thoughts go round and round in their heads but they are not taking action! And it is *action* that discharges arousal – in the same way that the act of drinking water when we are thirsty removes our feeling of thirst.

Worrying, therefore, puts heavy pressure on the REM sleep periods of the night as the brain tries to rid itself of that excessive load of emotional arousal by dreaming. What happens is very interesting. In people who aren't depressed, there is a proper balance between the stage of sleep in which the physical repair of our body tissues occurs and the stage in which we have most of our dreams

> **❝ Worrying puts heavy pressure on the REM sleep periods of the night ... ❞**

(REM sleep). We start the night with about 90 minutes of slow-wave body-repair sleep, which, among other things, tops up the energy we used during the day. (Dream sleep itself burns up a massive amount of energy, so we need energy even to dream.) Then, after 90 minutes, the first REM sleep period occurs and it lasts up to 10 minutes. As the night progresses, we have more REM sleep and less slow-wave sleep, culminating in about 30 or 40 minutes of REM sleep just before we wake up in the morning.

Depressed people, however, enter REM sleep much earlier in the night than non-depressed people and their dreams are more intense and last much longer. The first REM period of a depressed person starts between 20 and 50 minutes after falling asleep, when energy levels are still low, and can last for up to 50 minutes. That represents a vast draining of precious energy early on in the night. No wonder depressed people are always so exhausted. The balance between the energy-burning REM sleep and the recuperative slow-wave sleep is out of kilter.

It is this out-of-balance sleep pattern that causes the sleep problems that depressed people experience. Some wake up early, even though still tired, and some have difficulty dropping off to sleep as their thoughts go round and round, and some wake every couple of hours and have difficulty dropping off again. They all wake up exhausted and have struggle to motivate themselves to do anything much in the day. (This is the classic sleep pattern in depression. You probably recognise it.) But *why* can't they motivate themselves in the morning? To explain exactly what is going on here, we must look again at what happens in normal sleep.

Why depressed people have difficulty motivating themselves

We know from laboratory studies of brain waves that, just before we go into REM sleep, and while we are in it, powerful electrical signals in the brain pass through it like a wave, but very quickly. On electroencephalogram (EEG) recordings they appear as sudden spikes. For that reason the signal is often called a 'PGO wave' or a 'PGO spike' (the PGO standing for the initials of the structures of the brain it passes through). These waves constitute what is known as our 'orientation response' as they direct (or orientate) our attention towards anything that may be of importance to us. But, to keep things simple, it might be more helpful if we refer to it here as a 'buzzer'. Buzzers are also intended to attract our attention and that is the role of the PGO wave, both in sleep and when we are awake. When we are awake, this 'buzzer' attracts our attention to anything in our environment that changes – a sudden movement behind us, a burning smell, a loud noise, for instance. For our long-distant ancestors, living in the wild, reacting quickly to something like that would have made the difference between life and death. It still does for us today. We would not be able to drive cars the way we do without this mechanism orientating us to the constant changes in the environment. But the 'buzzer' also operates in more subtle circumstances – the same neural pathways fire when *anything* attracts our attention or interests us during the day.

When we are asleep, however, sensory information is largely blocked from reaching the brain. We can't see anything through our closed eyelids and we don't normally respond to sounds, smells or sensations, especially when we enter the REM state and our muscles are paralysed. So the 'buzzer' that keeps going off while we are asleep isn't alerting us to a rustling curtain or the cat jumping onto the bed – unless that noise or sensation wakes us up or becomes incorporated into our dream in metaphorical form. (For instance, if we are dreaming we are lying under a tree, the sensation of the cat jumping on to the bed might be incorporated into the dream as a squirrel leaping onto us.)

Most of the time, though, we don't register what is happening around us while we sleep, so it is in response to an internally generated 'buzzer' that we start to dream. The 'buzzer' is, in effect, a signal saying, "Something interesting is about to happen! Pay attention." But, as there is no information coming into the brain from the outside world, the only thing the brain can do in response to the signal is to release from its memory stores whatever it had been expecting to happen during the day but which hasn't happened yet – the unexpressed emotional arousals that still need to be completed. The act of dreaming, by metaphorically playing out those arousals and, in effect, fulfilling the day's unfulfilled expectations, discharges them and frees up the brain to deal with the next day's emotionally arousing concerns.

> **❝ Dreaming de-arouses our unexpressed emotional arousals – our worries and concerns – from the previous day. ❞**

Depressed people, because they worry so much, have so many concerns and expectations to be discharged that the PGO 'buzzer' starts going off intensely much earlier in the night, stopping only briefly and then starting up again, and going on for much longer periods each time. The high amount of discharging that is going on, in response to the continual setting off of the 'buzzer', not only reduces the level of arousal in the brain (as the process is intended to do) but actually exhausts it. We only have so much motivational energy and (as has been shown in experiments on sleeping cats), if that energy is used up by excessive dreaming, we end up exhausted.

> 66 If our motivational energy is used up by excessive dreaming, we end up exhausted. 99

So this is why many depressed people wake early and can't get back to sleep again, despite still feeling tired. Their brains are unable to 'take' any more emotional discharge by dreaming (normally, the couple of hours before we wake up is the time when we have our longest periods of REM sleep). The 'buzzer' has run out of charge, the 'battery' is flat, and it can't perform its normal waking role of alerting them to what is happening around them, so that they can switch attention from one task to another, see what needs doing and get interested in different things. So they remain in a slump, unable to motivate themselves to get going and fazed by the least little requirement, such as getting dressed, eating properly or making a phone call. In such a state, everything seems meaningless and not worth doing, and that, of course, is exactly how we experience the world when we are depressed.

So depressed people have a double whammy. Firstly they wake up exhausted because they have had too much energy-burning REM sleep and not enough recuperative (energising) slow-wave sleep. And, secondly, because the PGO 'buzzer' that orientates them to the world is so over-stimulated, they cannot motivate themselves to do anything. Since meaning comes from taking action in the world, this lack of motiva-

Why watching TV is exhausting

WE MENTIONED earlier that even watching TV is exhausting and you will now be able to understand why. Modern television relies increasingly on techniques such as cuts, edits, zooming in, panning out, sudden sounds and sudden images. These are means of continually grabbing back our attention – in other words, they keep setting the 'buzzer' off. Just as when too many emotionally arousing expectations to be discharged in dreams will cause the 'buzzer's' 'battery' to go flat, too many novel visual and sound effects, crowded one after another like this, will also wear it out. Indeed, research has now shown that people who watch a lot of television feel passive, tired and less able to concentrate afterwards, as if the television has somehow sucked their energy out of them. (And, indeed, it has!) Whereas mood tends to improve after taking part in sports or engaging in hobbies, it commonly worsens after watching TV for four hours or more. Clearly, spending long periods in front of the TV is a particularly bad idea when feeling depressed.

tional energy drains the meaning and purpose out of life. Every activity, thought or relationship seems empty and pointless.

Although the 'buzzer' gradually gets its battery recharged during the day, this doesn't help matters much. For when depressed people wake up, they go back into their interminable introspections and worries – made worse by the additional worry about why they feel so empty and tired and lacking in energy and interest – and so the same cycle is played out again that night, and the next, and the next and the next.

It should be clear, now, that it is the need to discharge the emotional arousal caused by negative thinking, running constantly through the brain, that leads to the increase in duration and intensity of REM sleep and it is this that triggers the whole cycle of depression. It should be equally clear that it is absolutely vital to shift out of this negative cast of mind, if you want to overcome depression. Fortunately, there are many ways that you can do this and we will go through them later in the book.

Depression lowers the immune system

As we mentioned earlier, when people are depressed, the blood levels of a stress hormone called cortisol rise steeply. Cortisol is the hormone that gets the body ready to deal with perceived dangers by fighting or fleeing – once the threat would have been a wild animal but now it might be an angry boss or a fear of failure. One side effect of so much of this hormone being released is a corresponding drop in the efficiency of the immune system. When our very survival appears to be at stake, it is more important to put our physical energy into getting our bodies ready to shift us quickly out of danger rather than to fight off infections. So, not surprisingly, the heightened stress of depression makes us repeatedly vulnerable to opportunistic infections, for instance from the viruses that cause colds. You will notice that, as your depression gets better, so does your ability to fight off common infections.

You don't need to feel worse before you feel better

Some people may tell you that, if you want to get better from depression, you need to surrender to it, explore your pain in depth and search for its root cause. This is untrue. So is the idea that depression is anger turned inward, which you therefore need to express – perhaps by pummelling pillows or shrieking abuse at a 'parent' you have to conjure up in your imagination to represent the one who made you have piano lessons or football practice against your will all those years ago. Yet this is what some counselling and psychotherapy currently on offer invites you to believe. We know of therapists who have said, in effect, when depressed clients complain that they are not feeling any better after many sessions of 'deep' digging, "You can't have dug deep enough, yet".

This is ludicrous, if you give it a moment's thought, and apply the understandings that we have just explained. Digging up emotional pains from the past – psychological archaeology – just increases your misery and gives you even more to worry and ruminate about, further disrupting your sleep and causing even more exhaustion and lack of motivation. The more emotionally aroused a person becomes by digging up painful memories from the past, the less able they are to engage the rational part of the brain. This might excuse *them* from realising that it is completely irrational to attempt to get better by getting worse first, but it doesn't excuse the therapists who encourage this sort of thing. However, such

> 66 Digging up emotional pains from the past just increases your misery ... 99

therapists are actually emotionally aroused too. They may even think it is part of their job to sob beside you. One therapist told us proudly that he got down on the floor with his patients to "enter their pain" and wail alongside them! This is so painful and draining for everyone concerned that such therapists have, in our presence, referred to themselves as "the wounded healers". (Of course they are not healing anybody.) Wouldn't we be surprised if doctors treating broken legs and arms broke their own first, so that they would know what their patients were going through? And imagine a doctor treating stomach pain by giving you something to *increase* it and then saying, "Yes, this will get to the root of it now!"

Not only does this approach not make sense when you think about it, but new understandings that neuroscientists have uncovered about the way the brain works confirm that encouraging painful memories is just about the worst thing to do for depression. We now know that the brain is almost infinitely malleable. What we think and how we feel makes a physical impression on it. The brain is a "trembling web of connected cells" as neuropsychologist Professor Ian Robertson memorably described it, and our experiences are literally re-sculpting our brains all the time.[12] When we stimulate and challenge our brains, new connections are forged; the more we use these (the more we practise skills or act on what we've learned), the stronger those connections grow.

Inevitably, then, this means that, if we continually focus our attention on the bad things that have happened to us in our past, or keep mentally revisiting a particular source of misery we are suffering in the present, we reinforce negative experi-ences at the expense of positive ones. It is a physiological cer-tainty! Far from 'getting it all out' when we delve into pain or repressed anger we actually deepen our depressive mood by going over and over morbid things. In effect, we are rehears-ing and perfecting depressive thinking, just as effectively as we can rehearse to strengthen a musical or sporting talent!

This finding from neuroscience explains the psychological finding that people with depression have either a better mem-ory for negative events and experiences or a poorer memory for positive events and experiences, and that repeatedly recall-ing negative information makes the depression worse and last longer.[13] And, as we have explained, going over painful feel-ings from the past also encourages brain exhaustion.

'Pattern matching' gone wrong

Digging up the past is dangerous for another reason, too. It can make us relate past experiences to present experiences in completely inappropriate ways.

When a certain image, place, action or sensation calls to mind another such image, place, action or sensation experienced in the past, people are doing what we call 'pattern matching'. In fact, we pattern match all the time but in such a tiny fraction of a nanosecond that we have no idea we are doing it. All new experiences, even the most mundane, are pattern matched and compared to what we know already. We see a chair and we recognise it as a chair because our memory stores produce a file marked 'chair' that tells us broadly what it looks like and what we can expect to use it for. This lets us know that it doesn't represent a threat and that we can sit on it. (If, however, it has two broken legs, it doesn't match our pattern for a sturdy chair and so we know not to sit on it.) All this, as we said, is instantaneous and unconscious. If such processes had to be conscious, we would never get anything done in the day.

Many pattern matches do reach consciousness, however. For instance, walking past a house, a man might suddenly smell the pungent, unusual aroma of roasting peppers, and instantly this experience brings to mind an aunt who used to roast peppers when he visited her as a boy in her country home. Or we see a tall woman with a floppy hat and it reminds us of an old, long forgotten acquaintance who was also extremely tall and wore a floppy hat when gardening. Pattern matching is a powerful facility of the brain. We use it to make sense of, and add to our understanding of, life, relating what is new to what we already know. We might say, "The sensation in my stomach was like going up in a lift" or "It was an animal that looked like a cat but was a lot bigger".

The reason that we are mentioning all this is that, when we are depressed or anxious, we are often drawing on *inappropriate* patterns. So a woman who was mentally or physically abused by a previous lover, who always used to start out acting lovingly and then sudden switched into abuse mode, may flinch every time her new partner says loving things to her or puts his arm around her. Her fear that the relationship will go wrong or that the partner is untrustworthy makes her act in a distant, rejecting way towards him. Hurt and spurned,

> 66 Pattern matching is a powerful facility of the brain. 99

the partner starts to back off and the relationship heads downhill, confirming the woman's belief that men can't be trusted and relationships don't work. Likewise, having been informed by one's partner in a restaurant that a relationship is over can be sufficient impetus for someone to develop a subsequent horror of restaurants, which they interpret as a phobia about eating in public. They may then become depressed, as their social lives shrink. (How to uncouple inappropriate pattern matches is something we will describe in Part 2 of this book.)

The problem in situations like these is that the wrong match has been made and consequently we behave in the present as if we are still dealing with a difficulty that is now way in the past. So experiencing misery and recalling, in therapy, a time when some disaster struck and you felt the same way as you do now, does not mean you should assume you never got over that disaster – any more than smelling roasting peppers means the man should visit his aunt. Just by recognising the pattern-matching process and understanding why an event or experience has come to mind can often be sufficient to remove the power from it.

Remember – the reasons for depression may have their *roots* in the past (perhaps an experience of sexual abuse, failing to 'fit in' at school or the loss, several years ago, of a loved one) but the depression exists only because, as a result, certain human needs (such as those for intimacy, attention, status or meaning) are not being met *now*.

Drugs are not the best or the quickest way to deal with depression

It is well established that antidepressant drugs can lift the symptoms of depression but they are not nearly as effective as your doctor, in all good faith, might have led you to believe. (Drug companies have done an excellent job in persuading doctors that the newest antidepressants are powerfully effective. But their own research shows that these drugs are no more effective than a well-delivered placebo.) Antidepressants take between four and six weeks to exert their maximum effects and resolve depressive symptoms in just a third of the people who take them; they help somewhat, in the case of another third; and the final third receive no benefit at all. Even when antidepressants do work, they don't prevent depression com-

---

A placebo in medicine is an inactive, harmless substance (often nicknamed a 'sugar pill') given to a patient by an authority they believe in, such as a doctor, who tells them it is a real medicinal drug.

The 'placebo effect' is the tendency for a people to get better because of the expectation created in them by taking the sugar pill. The psychological expectation transfers to, and mobilises, their own natural healing responses. Many complementary therapies work through the placebo effect, as does much orthodox medicine.

ing back again, in the way that good psychotherapy does (and the important word there is 'good'). Also, many people find that the side effects of drugs are so unpleasant that they would rather remain depressed than take the 'cure'.

More importantly, we now know that, far from being benign helpers, antidepressant drugs can be dangerous. Two years ago, the pharmaceutical company GlaxoSmithKline was obliged to admit that its bestselling drug, the antidepressant paroxetine, didn't cause unpleasant withdrawal effects in a mere two out of every thousand people who took it, as it had claimed, but actually induced these effects in seven out of every hundred users. The withdrawal effects included pins and needles sensations, dizziness and alarming, vivid dreams, as well as some cases of agitation and nausea. In some cases, a British psychiatrist reported, the effects were so severe that they could be treated only by re-starting the drug.

It has now come to light that taking antidepressants like paroxetine can even have serious long-term health consequences. Paroxetine is one of a group of antidepressants known as SSRIs (which stands for selective serotonin reuptake inhibitors), which raise serotonin availability in the body. As we have mentioned, serotonin is the brain chemical that has the effect of lifting mood. However, it is now so widely recognised that the drugs in this group can cause a worsening

...continued on page 58

Why claims for SSRIs may be overrated

IRONICALLY, psychiatrists were highly delighted by the SSRIs, when they came on the scene in the 1980s, because they appeared to cause fewer side effects than tricyclics, the anti-depressants in use at the time. This enthusiasm has been happily promoted by the drug companies, as the SSRIs are considerably more expensive. However, many researchers now question whether these drugs ever really did much of what they were supposed to do at all.

SSRIs are designed to affect levels of serotonin in the brain but only five per cent of serotonin is found in the brain; the rest is distributed throughout the body, to do things such as help regulate the digestion system, the pumping of blood around the body and the workings of the reproductive system. So the drugs affect a lot else besides serotonin levels in the brain. It could even be, according to some critics, that SSRIs don't really have an antidepressant effect at all but merely a general calming down effect.

We can see that there are clear grounds for this concern if we look at the way that SSRIs ended up on the market.

When new drugs are developed, they have to be tested in rigorously controlled clinical trials, in which usually the efficacy of the new drug is compared with that of a placebo (a dummy drug). This means ensuring that neither the doctors prescribing the drugs nor the patients taking them know who is receiving which (a procedure called 'blinding'). This is important because, if either doctors or patients know which is being taken, then the 'placebo effect' may occur. This is when our own expectation

of getting better (through the new drug) has the effect of stimulating our internal healing powers, rather than, or as well as,
recovery due to the drug. (Conversely, disappointment at realising we are on a dummy pill is likely to reduce our expectation of
getting better, and thus damp down any natural healing power.)

But, just as there are legal loopholes for avoiding payment of
the due amount of tax, so there are legal ways of manipulating
the placebo effect to make a drug look more effective than it
really is. For instance, in trials using a placebo drug and an
active drug, experimenters carrying out the trial on behalf of
the drug company may use 'placebo washout' procedures. This
means that everyone is given the placebo first and all those who
get significantly better are taken out of the trial at that point.
Then the people who are left are given either the placebo or
the real drug. The effect, of course, is that the experimenters
already know that those on the placebo aren't so likely to do very
well, as they are the ones whose symptoms didn't get better
the first time they had a placebo. So, when their wellness is compared with that of people who took the real drug, it will make the
drug look a lot more effective than perhaps it really is.

To give an example, 100 people enter the trial and all are
given a placebo. Of these, 20 get better and are removed from
the trial. The remaining 80 are divided into two groups, half
receiving the placebo and half the drug. Five of those on the
placebo get better and 30 of those on the drug. It looks as if the
drug is six times better than the placebo. In fact, counting in
all the people who started the trial, it is not much better than
the placebo at all – 25 getting better on the placebo and 30 ▶

on the drug.

It might even be the case that many people in trials do realise when they are taking an active drug (perhaps they experience particular side effects) and so their expectation of getting better may be partly responsible anyway. Recently some researchers looked at 191 double-blind placebo-controlled trials (selected at random from trials published in five leading general medical journals and in psychiatry journals), and found that researchers in just 15 of the trials made checks on whether blinding had worked. In just five trials was blinding claimed to be successful and for only two of those five trials was any evidence presented to justify the claim of success![15]

The likelihood that antidepressant effectiveness may be over-rated is strengthened by another important piece of evidence. Trials that do not find a new drug significantly more effective than placebo usually go unpublished. When researchers took advantage of the American freedom of information laws to look at both published and unpublished trials, they found that the overall reduction in symptoms in more than 20,000 people who took part in trials was 40 per cent for antidepressants and 30 per cent for placebo. A survey of 50 trials showed that 54 per cent of people benefited from antidepressants but 46 per cent did not.[16] Just recently, researchers in Iceland collected nation-wide data on the prescribing of antidepressant drugs and on people's recovery from mental illnesses. They found that sales of antidepressants went up by over 16 per cent a year after SSRIs were introduced into Iceland but that there was no notice-able impact on psychiatric health at all.[17]

of symptoms and the development of violent or suicidal thoughts that the Food and Drug Adminstration in America wants clear warnings put on their labels.

Respected Harvard psychiatrist Dr Joseph Glenmullen trawled through a mountain of psychiatric journals and found evidence of thousands of cases of neurological side effects occurring with SSRIs. These included tics such as eye and lip twitching, agitation, severe restlessness, muscle spasms ranging from mild to severe (body parts becoming locked) and Parkinsonism.[14] He points out that all of these side effects were also caused in people prescribed major tranquillisers – drugs which, decades ago, used to be prescribed even to children for symptoms such as mild anxiety, insomnia and hyperactivity. Indeed, in 2004, safety worries led the UK government's Committee on Safety of Medicines to recommend that some SSRIs are not given to children under the age of 18 and others are still under review.

Because withdrawal effects of SSRIs may include symptoms similar to the symptoms of depression, such as fatigue and apathy, doctors often assume, when patients complain of them, that the depression hasn't lifted yet and prescribe the drug for longer. Be aware if this might be the case for you.

SSRIs may be even less effective than they are claimed to be. (If you are interested in knowing why, see the panel on page 55.) **But, if you are taking an antidepressant, do not just stop taking them. It is very important to withdraw gradually,** to reduce as far as possible the likelihood of painful and damaging withdrawal symptoms.

Why some people *do* respond better to anti-depressants than to psychotherapy

There are some depressed people, albeit a very small minority, who respond better to antidepressants than to psychological interventions. For instance, people on the autistic spectrum with Asperger's syndrome (a less severe form of autism) fall into this category. They may be highly intelligent but have difficulties connecting emotionally with others and with juggling multiple priorities in their minds simultaneously. Because of their 'straight line' thinking, they find unexpected changes in their environment stressful and this can lead to depression.

However, psychotherapy is difficult for them because of their highly literal and rigid thinking style. They can't usually be helped to make the important imaginative leap that would enable them to shift their perspective and view their problems in a less limiting way or, even if they can take that leap, it may not trigger the changes in their physiology that would bring down their stress levels as easily as they would for most other people. This can leave them trapped in a Catch-22 situation – they can't deal with whatever new challenge they are facing until their depression lifts but their depression won't lift until they actually 'see' themselves dealing with the new challenge. Antidepressants can help break this vicious circle.

Postnatal depression is no different from ordinary depression

Up to 15 per cent of women develop depression after giving birth. In the case of one or two per cent of women, the depression may become psychotic – taking the form of hallucinations and delusions, which can put the baby's life, as well as their own, at risk. Postnatal depression (or postpartum depression, as doctors may call it) is often viewed as a biologically-based condition, attributable to a high level of hormonal imbalance after childbirth.

In fact, surprising as it may sound, there is no evidence that the majority of postnatal depression is due to hormonal imbalance. Indeed, the depression tends to develop weeks or months after the birth, by which time hormone levels are likely to be back to normal. ('Baby blues', on the other hand, a brief period of becoming over-emotional and tearful for no clear cause, which may occur a few days after a birth, is indeed hormone-induced and passes extremely quickly.) However, the fact that depression after childbirth is given the name 'postnatal depression' creates the impression that it is a distinct entity, just as would be the case if doctors commonly diagnosed 'redundancy depression' or 'bereavement depression' or 'being jilted depression', or even 'not winning the lottery depression'. Quite obviously, of course, these are simply circumstances that may trigger depression, and childbirth, in this respect, is no different.

(There is one important exception, however. In a very small proportion of women who suffer serious postnatal depression, the trigger is a disorder in which the body makes antibodies against its own thyroid gland. About 11 per cent of women are thought to make thyroid antibodies and this puts them at particularly high risk of postnatal depression, as well as damage to the thyroid gland. A simple test can detect whether this is the cause and treatment with the thyroid hormone thyroxine should resolve both problems. If women are found, during pregnancy, to be producing thyroid antibodies, treatment with thyroxine after the birth may prevent the development of depression altogether.)

> 66 Surprising as it may sound, there is no evidence that the majority of postnatal depression is due to hormonal imbalance. 99

Women who are most likely to develop depression after childbirth are those who have little support from a partner, family or friends and who are managing in highly stressful circumstances. For instance, a woman who is coping alone with a baby and three other young children in a high-rise flat is at raised risk of depression. However, as we said earlier, it is attitude and response to circumstances that determines whether a person sinks into depression, rather than those circumstances themselves. A woman could be in a happy relationship, living in a lovely home, enjoying a fully-paid career break and with her mother on hand to offer help, and still experience depression if she hasn't come to realistic terms with the big changes in life that a baby brings.

Inevitably, motherhood creates enormous changes that are demanding to cope with. (So does fatherhood – fathers may also suffer from depression after childbirth, particularly if their partner is depressed, but the problem often goes un-recognised.) As we have seen, sleep deprivation, which is an unavoidable part of new motherhood, will lower resistance, physically and emotionally, and increase vulnerability to low mood. And even when they are asleep new mothers tend not to sleep deeply (as they are subconsciously keeping an ear open for their baby) and therefore they often miss out on the important restorative Stage 4 sleep (as is often also the case with doctors and nurses who are on call).

So not only are new mothers getting less sleep than usual, the sleep they do get is unbalanced, with proportionately more REM sleep and less restorative, slow-wave sleep. This lack of balance invariably leads to brain exhaustion (itself another cause for worry) which, in turn, both makes it harder for the new mothers to think clearly about the emotionally-arousing concerns they have about their new life changes and increases their vulnerability to those worries. Thus their disrupted sleep can be both a symptom and a partial cause of any resulting depression.

Once they have established a routine and life settles down more, most new mothers recover quickly and are soon enjoying their new lives. However, others may find it harder to do so and the depression can become prolonged – many new mothers, for instance, may be at home during the day for the first time in years and therefore have all the more time to give way to any emotionally-arousing introspections and worries that they might have.

Women who tend towards having an emotionally driven black-and-white thinking style will find it more difficult to come to terms with the major changes and the uncertainties that becoming a parent entails – "Can I cope or can't I?" Concerns are likely to include worries about the baby's health and safety but equally powerful is the psychological shock of new motherhood and the realisation of its full implications. It may be difficult to reconcile fantasies of a life wonderfully transformed by the addition of a child with the reality of pacing the floor with a colicky, crying baby, worrying about being a failure as a parent. New mothers may feel consumed by their baby's needs and that they have lost their own sense of identity, as a working woman or as an independent person, and consequently their standing or status in the eyes of others.

As might be expected from what we've explained so far, women who become depressed after childbirth commonly have unrealistically high expectations of themselves. They think they should be able to meet all their baby's needs, without resentment or frustration, keep the home as clean as it used to be, cook meals for their partner and be loving, attentive – and perhaps even look sexually alluring, too – when that partner returns home after work. It is such perfectionism and all-or-nothing thinking, which, as we have seen, exacerbates the likelihood of depression.

If new mothers cannot easily, or are too despondent to, get out and spend time with other people, the important need for social connection will not be met. (Also, those who meet other new mothers in support groups are likely to feel far less isolated and become more confident of their own mothering abilities, as a result of sharing their anxieties and learning new skills.) Sometimes, in meeting a new baby's demanding schedule, new mothers may have little time to take care of their appearance in the way that they used to, and may snatch unhealthy snacks instead of eating properly. (A lack of certain nutriments, especially omega-3, can also make new mothers vulnerable to depression as we shall see in Part 2.) Considering themselves unattractive or overweight can easily lower self-esteem further. Worries about whether they are still attractive to their partners or about why they don't want sex (a common problem, when exhausted), add to the other ruminations likely to be going round and round in their heads and further disrupt sleep.

Postnatal depression can recur, after another birth, for the same reasons that any depression recurs: the psychological response to the circumstance (feeling anxious, isolated, and worrying about it all) is the same. If, however, a mother feels more confident and has more of a 'life' in place by the time the second baby arrives, postnatal depression is less likely.

Seasonal Affective Disorder (SAD)

SAD, or winter depression, can be triggered by reduced exposure to sunlight. Just as flowers turn to face the sunlight everyday, the brains of animals (ourselves included) are designed to respond to the changing patterns of sunlight associated with the different seasons of the year. When winter comes, many animals respond to the reducing amounts of sunlight by closing down and hibernating.

Sunlight directly influences levels of certain hormones, notably melatonin, related to sleep, mood and energy levels. About one in three people notices a drop in mood in the shortening days of winter. Ordinary artificial light is many times less strong than sunlight on even a cloudy day. Getting the right amount of light is a human need.

Fortunately, light boxes that can provide the extra light required, in as little as half an hour a day, are now readily available. Some light boxes even simulate dawn and gradually wake up users with the right amount of light to stimulate the correct hormone levels. The use of light boxes has proved very effective for people suffering from SAD.*

Even manic depression can sometimes be managed without drugs

Manic depression is a condition of self-absorption in which the sufferer swings between extreme highs and lows of mood. (The correct medical term is bipolar affective disorder.)

It is thought to be largely genetic in origin and, unlike ordinary depression, which affects over twice as many women as men, it affects men and women equally. Conventional treatment is with a drug called lithium, which appears to help regulate the emotions so as to prevent the huge swings between highly energetic euphoria and deep, disabling inertia. Very many people find lithium treatment highly effective and are able to live largely normal lives because of it; others find it does not help them at all and balk at its side effects, such as digestive disturbances, tremor and weight gain. Long-term use can also increase risk of kidney problems.

Manic depression can take a variety of forms. Some people

---

* One reputable source is Outside In Ltd, based in Cambridge. They can be contacted via: www.outsidein.co.uk

swing fairly regularly between mania and depression. Others experience relatively rare episodes of mania and extended bouts of depression, or vice versa. In those who mainly experience depression, manic depression may not be diagnosed for a long time.

Both states are, however, explicable in terms of the consequences of REM sleep disturbance. During their depressed phases, people with manic depression ruminate and worry too much, like anyone else with depression, ending up having proportionately much more REM sleep than tissue repair sleep, and waking up exhausted and listless.

In manic phases, however, they don't have enough sleep of any kind. They tend to want to stay awake late, cooking up what seem to them to be amazing schemes, taking on too many projects, or urgently cleaning the house from top to bottom or phoning all over the world. During the day, they are just as driven, using up phenomenal amounts of energy in all kinds of irrational pursuits. Inevitably, without sufficient REM sleep to discharge this intense, ongoing emotional arousal, they can keep this pace up only so long before crashing down to earth, heavily and hard. They then experience a high amount of compensatory REM sleep, worry and ruminate about why they have no energy and life is no fun, and the cycle of depression begins.

In many ways, manic depression is the all-or-nothing thinking style of the emotional brain writ large. When someone is manic, life is just too rosy; everything, they firmly believe, will go according to their plans, and nothing can disturb their optimism and enthusiasm. The experience can also be dizzyingly frightening, because of the speed the brain is functioning at and the grandeur of the delusions – as well as an awareness at some level that they are acting in a way that is totally out of control and often dangerous. When people crash from mania into depression, their mood is of the deepest despair imaginable, empty and black, and they are pessimistic about absolutely everything. Gone, in either phase, is the ability to contemplate the variety of shades of grey in between.

We have helped many people with manic depression. Some have achieved a normal life through a combination of drugs and human givens therapy. A few have managed to gain control of the condition without medication at all, or have tried medication before, and found it didn't help, but can now handle their mood swings, having understood how to make sense of them. If you are manic depressive and have found drugs don't help or you don't want to use them, it is important to identify the sort of stresses that, for you, precipitate a reaction that sets off mania or depression, and then ensure you act in a way that will avert it. We look at how to do this in the second part of this book.

Why more women suffer depression than men but men respond more drastically

It is a long-established fact that at least twice as many women as men are likely to suffer depression. Half of all women and a quarter of all men will suffer it at some time in their lives. That translates, according to a pooling of statistics from different sources, as roughly two to three per cent of men and four to nine per cent of women being depressed at any one time – a huge amount of misery, made up of the suffering of countless individuals. To this has to be added the much larger numbers, millions of people, family members, friends and colleagues of sufferers who are affected by their distress.

There are many reasons that explain why women might be more vulnerable, including the heavier 'daily life' burden that they tend to have to shoulder. Repeatedly, surveys show that, even when women work long hours full-time in a job or career, in general they still take on the lion's share of the domestic and child-rearing duties. Efforts to juggle and 'have it all' easily serve to send stress levels soaring. Failing to be 'superwoman-cum-supermums' may increase vulnerability to depression in many women, particularly those with a black-and-white thinking, perfectionist approach to life.

Clearly, it helps if women can create a better balance in their lives, one that comes closer to meeting their own emotional needs, as well as those of others they share their lives with. But this may not ever be entirely possible until a more supportive attitude exists in the workplace towards mothers, and both men and women's expectations change about how domestic duties and childcare should be shared when both partners are working. (There may actually be some physiological reasons for how such a disparity came about. Because of the way their brains are organised, as a general rule men are less able to spread their attention and so are less able to manage to juggle several things at once.)

> 66 Roughly 2–3% of men and 4–9% of women are depressed at any one time ... 99

However, it is not only in women with partners and children that the risk of depression rises. As we know, the biggest increase is in the younger age groups, often among childless single women. In fact what may largely explain women's greater vulnerability to depression are the natural psychological and biological differences between men and women.

Psychologist Simon Baron-Cohen, a professor at Cambridge University, has made a compelling case that men tend to be 'systemisers' while women are more usually 'empathisers'.[18] This means men, on average, have a drive to find out how systems work and to explore them (not necessarily mechanical things but also other complex systems, such as nature, politics, economics or the world of ideas); women more naturally excel at tuning into others' thoughts and being aware of and responsive to the feelings of others. As ever in these things, this is a generalisation. There are many individual men who are more empathiser than systemiser and many women who are more systemiser than empathiser. But it is a generalisation that is based on scientific knowledge about the structure of the brain.

It is more natural to women, because of their greater empathising skills, to want to explore their feelings, talk about them and analyse what is going on in their relationships and the rest of their lives, and to try to make sense of negative nuances. Of course, this means that they are more likely to ruminate and agonise over what isn't working, with the effect that their sleep becomes disturbed and the cycle of depression sets in. This also explains why women not only suffer from depression at least twice as frequently as men but why it takes them, on average, 50 per cent longer to recover from a depressive period.

Men, on the other hand, when they feel emotional, want to take immediate action to calm themselves down. The last thing a man wants to do is talk through the emotion in the way that a woman would because that would only increase the unpleasant feelings, raise his blood pressure, and, if he made a habit of it, damage his heart and health. Most men feel instinctively that they shouldn't 'get more in touch with their emotions' at all. If a man can't solve a problem or situation that is upsetting him straight away he is more likely to distance himself from it by walking out. Failing that, he might try to suppress the emotional pain by means of working too hard or drinking too much, or by indulging in excessive physical activity, such as sport, to let off steam.

In general, men's systemising bent leads them to direct their energies into problem solving rather than an analysis of their emotions. This, too, can have its downside in terms of depression. For, when men become severely depressed and are in the grip of the black-and-white thinking style of the brain, they are more likely to decide that their situation is completely hopeless and that they must do something to find a way out of it. They go into problem-solving mode. And one obvious 'solution' to the problem is to end it all. But these men are by now too emotional to see the absurdity of this permanent solution to a temporary problem. This is why three times more men than women succeed in committing suicide.

Why relationships can be depressing

Women and men often feel poles apart from each other in relationships, in terms of understanding how the other feels and thinks. This is not so very far from the truth. In women, a physical channel (called the corpus callosum), that links the left and right hemispheres of the brain creates greater communication between them. The left hemisphere of the brain is more concerned with logical, analytical, rational activity, while the right is more intuitive and emotional – although both hemispheres are involved to some degree in most mental activities and emotional reactions. What this greater communication between hemispheres is thought to mean is that women's emotional awareness is acute, whatever they are doing, whereas men are more able to compartmentalise the emotional and practical sides of their lives – or in fact can't help doing so.

This has advantages and disadvantages for both sexes. For instance, women may be better judges of character, as they are more aware of non-verbal signals, such as body language and tone of voice. On other occasions, however, feeling an emotional connection may cloud judgement. Men may be less able than women to read an interpersonal situation but are better able to shut out emotional distractions and get on with whatever task is in hand.

We know, from experiments, that such differences are real. For instance, from the age of three, girls are better able than boys to recognise the emotion expressed by a facial expression (angry, sad, happy, etc.) and this superiority persists right through childhood into adulthood. Boys have greater trouble with emotions almost right from the start. They are more emotionally demanding of their mothers as babies and appear to be less sensitive to the distress of others. In one telling experiment, six-year-old boys listening on a two-way baby monitor to what they thought was a baby crying were more likely to turn the monitor off, whereas girls attempted to soothe the 'baby'. But what seemed to be indifference on the boys' part was in fact something else: their heart rates and stress levels were much higher than those of the girls, showing significantly greater anxiety. They couldn't bear the baby's distress – or their own. In other words, they were *more* sensitive to it.

> " During a fierce argument, a man's blood pressure and heart rate rise much higher than a woman's do ... "

This tells us something very important about male emotions, which could account for a lot of the distress that men and women experience in problematic relationships. Men have a lower emotional threshold. They simply cannot tolerate too much emotional arousal. (When families break up, it is boys who are the most highly distressed.) Because their nervous systems are more sensitive to stress than women's, and take longer to settle down after emotional upset, in the interests of survival they must suppress or override their emotions, to a certain extent. This explains why, to women's frequent amazement, in the middle of a heated argument, a man can just walk out of the room or appear to 'turn off' and refuse to engage, while the woman is still churned up with feelings that she is desperate to talk about. During a fierce argument, a man's blood pressure and heart rate rise much higher than a woman's do and, if he doesn't take steps to calm himself down, he could be in danger of a heart attack or a violent outburst. So, unless he can reduce the level of emotion by taking immediate action, he tends to avoid confrontation. Women, on the other hand, need to express their emotions in order to defuse them. If they are continually left in a state of emotional arousal, because their partners won't engage, it is not surprising if depression ensues.

This important difference in the way men and women handle emotional expression is at the heart of a vast amount of modern marital discord. We have found, in our work with couples, that just helping men and women to understand these differences can be highly useful in enabling them to adjust their expectations of each other, and settle on calmer ways to negotiate their way around difficulties, or at least be more tolerant of the opposite sex.

Families suffer too

Depression, in its way, can be contagious. Seeing someone you love in a state of abject misery, lacking all interest in life, is highly likely to cause distress. When a man is depressed and is even less communicative and more withdrawn into himself than usual, his wife may despair as to how to help him. Her natural way is to want to talk to him and explore with him how he is feeling, and what the matter is, while he will probably just want to be left entirely alone. She may well feel guilty and full of self-blame, if she cannot help him.

A man with a depressed wife, on the other hand, may respond in the problem-solving thinking style that is familiar to him, and, at first, want to come up with solutions for every grief his wife pours out to him. "You are still distraught about your mother's death. Let's take a holiday. You haven't the energy to walk down the road? Let's go in the car, then." If his well-meaning solutions and advice are repeatedly rejected or ignored, he may then withdraw emotionally or even become depressed himself.

Depressed mothers, being locked into their own misery, are very often unable to meet the needs of their children, emotionally and sometimes even physically. Also, children are sensitive to the moods of their parents. If you have, or had, a depressive mother or father yourself, you may well think that you have inherited a depressive 'gene'. As we said earlier, no gene for depression has ever been identified. But you may well have picked up from your depressed parent something of their pessimistic view of the world – "nothing goes the way you want it to"; "it's not worth bothering", "you can't trust people", "let's not make an effort because it won't come to anything" – and have 'learned' your own emotional responses from them.

In at least 50 per cent of cases, family relationships are damaged by depression. We have often had to treat depressed partners of depressed clients.

If you are reading this book because someone you care about has depression, you can see that it is important to look after yourself emotionally, as well as trying to look after them. The suggestions we make in the next section for helping people to get their needs met are, in most cases, just as relevant for you as for anyone you are trying to care for.

PART 2

How to lift depression

$\mathscr{N}$OW that you truly understand what causes depression and why it takes the form it does, you should find that you are much more ready and able to make the changes that will lift it.

We have worked with countless depressed people over the past 20 years. A great many of them have come to see us only because their distressed relatives have persuaded them to. They have arrived, feeling hopeless and thinking the therapy will be pointless, perhaps unwilling or even unable to speak or meet our eyes. Very many have previously made one or more suicide attempts and have been patients in psychiatric hospitals, often several times. Yet most have come out of their deep depression quickly (and very often feel significantly better after just one session.) This is because we work with the givens of human nature. That is the heart of the human givens approach.

So what are the human givens?

To live successful and fulfilled lives we all need to have certain basic needs met and, to help us get them met, nature also gave us inherent abilities and skills (innate resources). Because all babies come into the world with these needs and resources we call them human givens. They are our genetic inheritance.

It is an obvious 'given', for instance, that, to thrive, we need to have food, water, warmth and shelter from the elements. But there are many other needs, emotional rather than physical, that are equally crucial for our well-being – and sometimes even for survival. These include the needs for:

- security: a sense of having a safe territory around us so we can lead our lives without undue fear and enjoy privacy whenever necessary

- volition: a sense of autonomy and control over our lives

- attention: receiving it from others, but also giving it

- emotional connection to others: friendship, intimacy

- connection to the wider community: being part of something larger than ourselves

- a sense of status: knowing that we have a valued place in each of the different social groups we belong to

- a sense of competence and achievement: which ensures

we don't suffer from 'low self-esteem'

- a sense of meaning and purpose: which comes from
  being mentally and/or physically stretched

We know these needs – love, sense of control, status, etc – are important because much research shows that a lack of any one of them, over a period of time, takes a major toll on our physical and mental health. But all of these needs have to be met in a balanced way: too much attention, for example, is as bad as too little. And a life lived in total safety without risk can be as harmful as one lived in a state of insecurity (because it makes us soft, vulnerable and incompetent in the face of real danger). We all have to be ready for the unexpected. The one certainty in life is that change happens.

To help us find ways to meet our needs, nature has given us a wealth of resources, such as:

- the ability to learn and remember

- the ability to build rapport, empathise and connect
  with others

- a powerful imagination

- an ability to think things out, to analyse, plan and adapt

- an ability to understand the world unconsciously:
  through pattern matching

- the ability to step back into our 'observing self': and thus
  be objective

– the ability to dream: and thereby discharge any
unexpressed, emotionally arousing expectations so we
can face each new day afresh.

These needs and resources together – the human givens – are
in-built patterns, or biological templates, which direct our
actions and responses.

If any needs are seriously unmet, or any of our innate
resources are damaged, missing or used incorrectly (whether
we realise it or not) we suffer mental distress; typically we get
anxious, angry or depressed.[19]

For instance, healthy babies are born with the ability to
build rapport with the person who will be their prime carer.
They enchant us with their ability to mimic facial expressions
or movements, some of which they can do within hours of
birth. In doing so, they help build the bonds between themselves and the person they are initially dependent on for the
meeting of their every need. But if a child lacks that skill, as
autistic children do, it is far harder for them to negotiate a
way through the world.

We yearn for connection with others and for intimacy, yet,
if our parents were cold towards us, or neglectful, or even
overly demanding and critical, we may find it hard to trust
others and so fail to form relationships that last. Or, because
of particular circumstances, we may not have had the chance
to develop certain necessary skills that other people uncon-

sciously use to connect with each other – the ability to make small talk, to be interested in what the other person has to say, to give and accept compliments and so forth.

Human givens therapists work by looking to see which of these important needs are unmet in people's lives and/or what resources are either not being used at all or are being used incorrectly. We then help a person build up effective ways to meet their needs. These are the techniques we are going to share with you. (When we talk about 'you', we mean the person who is depressed, but the information can also be put to use by friends and family, to help a depressed person and themselves.)

Learn how to calm yourself down

You may not feel as if you are in a highly aroused state but, if you are deeply depressed, your stress hormones are circulating like crazy. You are locked into your emotional brain and, as we've seen, that stops you from thinking clearly. Everything is reduced to black-or-white terms. Life must be perfect or else it is a catastrophe. You need to get back a sense of perspective if you are hoping to deal with your depression and that can't be done while you are emotionally aroused. One of the first things a human givens therapist will do, after gathering information from someone about what is going on in their life and why they are seeking help, is calm them down. Most people find this an enormously helpful experience – like being given permission to stop agonising and ruminating, and just appreciate being alive again ... like a happy child. We are often told, after we have relaxed someone, that it is the first time they have felt that way in years. And it *is* remarkable – people always look and feel younger afterwards.

You may think, especially if you have anxiety-driven depression, that you could never possibly relax. We haven't come across anyone who couldn't be helped to relax, even people sunk deeply into depression and completely dismissive of the possibility of change. Ivan once relaxed someone who was depressed because he had Parkinson's disease. The man was pacing up and down, literally shaking from head to toe, as the tension and anxiety were exacerbating his symptoms so much. Within minutes he became so calm and still that he could suddenly see his life and condition in an entirely new light and come out of his low mood.

> **" A few minutes' calm is a wonderful gift to give yourself. "**

It is natural for the body to want relief from the highly unnatural state of unrelenting stress. Ten or 15 or 30 minutes' calm is a wonderful gift to give yourself. It will show you, through the very experience of changes you can induce in your own body, that things *can* be different; you *can* make changes happen. (If you are unable to do this for yourself at the beginning, you may benefit from seeing a therapist who can do a guided relaxation with you. We often tape such sessions, so clients can replay the tape and induce a relaxed state whenever they want to.)

Three ways to relax quickly

The following techniques are easy to learn. Although it may help the first time you try them for someone else to talk you through the steps (so that you can focus on relaxing) this isn't essential as they are easy to remember so that you can do them on your own whenever you need to.

1. Many people find that the easiest way to relax is to concentrate on their own breathing, so we suggest you practise this method first.

- Settle yourself comfortably somewhere that you won't be disturbed. Make sure your clothes are loose.

- Sit or lie comfortably with your hands side by side in your lap, or your arms by your side, and your legs uncrossed.

- Close your eyes.

- Now concentrate on becoming aware of your feet on the floor, of your legs and arms, wherever they are resting, and your head against the cushion, pillow or chair back.

- Then begin to make each out-breath last longer than your in-breath. (This works because the out-breath stimulates the body's natural relaxation response, the parasympath-etic nervous system. By changing your pattern of breathing in this way, your body automatically begins to relax.) A good way to do this is to breathe in to the count of 7, then breathe out gently and more slowly to the count of 11. Do this about 10 to 20 times, knowing that you will relax more each time.

- Concentrate on the counting (don't let your mind wander off) and feel the welcome sense of calm gradually flow in.

- Try and be aware of how much less tense you feel, just by relaxing your breathing and blocking out your worrying thoughts.

This 7/11 technique, as it's known, is good for instant relax-ation too. Just do it a few times, wherever you are, if you feel so wound up that you can't make a simple decision, or are nervous, or want to burst into tears. (If you find it easier, substitute 3/5 for 7/11. The important thing is that your out-breaths last longer than your in-breaths.)

2. Another good way to relax is to settle yourself comfortably, then make your hands into the tightest fists possible. (But only use this method if you have healthy hands.)

- Look at your fists carefully as you squeeze them harder and harder, being aware of the whiteness of the knuckles, the feeling of your nails against your palms, the pressure of your thumbs against your forefingers, the rigidity of your wrists and the tension in your elbows.

- Keep squeezing your fists like this and concentrate on the physical sensations for a minute or two. To help you concentrate, close your eyes.

- Then, with all your attention focused on your hands, allow your hands to slowly unwind and relax.

- Still with your eyes closed feel the enjoyable sensation spreading quite naturally through your fingers and up along your arms as the tension drains away. You may find it takes the form of whatever your body needs – coolness if you tend to be too hot or warmth if you tend to feel too cold – or else you might just feel a pleasant tingling sensation.

- Whatever form it takes, let the relaxing sensation spread on through your body, smoothing your brow, your cheek muscles, your jaw, your shoulders, chest and so on, down to your toes.

- Keep your focus on the falling away of stress and the calming differences you can sense in your body.

- You can repeat this for as long as you like, simply enjoying and noticing the calming changes that will occur throughout your body.

3. The third highly effective method, like the previous one, is derived from yoga and achieves relaxation in a similar way.

• Work gradually through the main muscles of your body, tensing each in turn for a count of 10 and then relaxing them. As in the previous technique, it works on the simple mechanical principle that, if you tense muscles and then relax them, your muscles are always more relaxed afterwards than before you tensed them.

• Try starting with your feet, move up to your calf muscles, then your knees, your thighs, your tummy muscles and so on.*

Create a 'safe and special place'

You can make relaxing an even more pleasant experience by using the time with your eyes closed to waft yourself away mentally to some pleasant imaginary place, or to a real place that you love to go to. People often choose to imagine themselves walking on empty beaches by the sea, or in the mountains, or by a stream, or sitting in a beautiful garden. You can make the scene whatever you want it to be, tranquil or lively. Perhaps you are more relaxed when there are other people around, so incorporate their presence into your imaginings.

---

* A hugely helpful relaxation CD (called 'Relax'), with all of the above information and much more, is available from the publishers of this book. Call: +44 (0)1323 811662 for details or visit: www.hgonline.co.uk/shop/

Perhaps you relax through a sporting activity, such as playing football or squash, or cycling or swimming or walking in the hills, in which case visualise yourself enjoying doing it. Wherever you choose, and whatever you choose to do there, concentrate on making the occasion as real as it can be. If you are good at visualising things in your mind's eye, really *see* the colours of the flowers or the trees or the grass. *Hear* the sounds – the gentle whoosh of rippling waves, the rustling of leaves, the voices of people enjoying themselves. *Feel* the textures; *smell* the smells.

Imagine your chosen scene in detail, so that you can make it your 'special, safe place', one you will always be able to call to mind and enjoy when relaxed – or to help you relax quickly.

Calm yourself down in one of these ways whenever you start becoming overwhelmed with feelings. Just as you can't contract and relax a muscle at the same time, so you can't be anxious when you are in a relaxed state. When you are calm and free from pressing thoughts, even for a short period, you have access to the rational part of your brain and can more clearly recognise and question your black-and-white thinking.

> 66 Calm yourself down whenever you start becoming overwhelmed with feelings. 99

Do an emotional 'needs audit' on yourself

If people's lives are going well, they do not get depressed. People get depressed only if fundamental needs are not being met – either because of circumstances or because of unwitting misuse of innate resources. It follows therefore that it is important to clearly identify what is not going right in your life at the moment, so that you can take some practical steps to deal with it.

EXERCISE:

When you have calmed yourself down and are in a more relaxed state of mind, try to take stock. Think back to when you became depressed (this time around, if you have been depressed before) and see if you can recall what was happening in your life at the time. Was anything upsetting or bothering you? (If you are trying to help someone else who is depressed, you may have some ideas yourself – for instance the depression may have developed after the death of someone close or after the loss of a job or the development of a health problem.) Then think about what is happening now in your life and go through the list of needs below one by one.

Try to be as honest and probing as you can, when answering these questions. If you let your depression do the audit, it will probably conclude, "Nothing is working. None of my needs is being met!" But that is black-and-white thinking, and isn't true. If you find this is your reaction, bring in a sensible friend, someone who knows you well, to help you do the audit. You may find, when you look hard, that many parts of your life are (or could be) working very well, but you are letting one unsatisfactory aspect govern it all.

If you find doing this needs audit difficult, to make it easier, think carefully about just one or two of them at a time. Work your way through the list over a time period you can cope with, all the while looking for reasonable ways to get as many of your needs met as possible.

And remember, no life is going to be ideal.

Do you feel safe?

For instance, are you confident at work or do you feel undermined by your peers or your boss? Do you dread social occasions where you don't know anyone? Are you being bullied? Have you been assaulted on the street or within a relationship and fear a recurrence? Is your livelihood or home at risk? Do your fears prevent you from doing things that you want to do? Do physical illness and pain make you feel insecure and cause you to worry? Do you feel vulnerable because you are older and weaker than you once were?

Do you have people in your life who are important to you and to whom you are important?

Or have you experienced loss? For instance, has a serious relationship recently ended? Are you grieving for someone who has died? (Bereavement, understandably, can make us feel sad and bereft, but if you are still completely grief-stricken over someone who died at least two years ago, that is no longer normal grieving.) Have you lost touch with friends or stopped seeing them lately? Is there at least one person with whom you can be yourself, have fun and share your joys and anxieties?

Do you have wider connections?

For instance, do you know people outside of close family and close friends? Do you help others, such as neighbours or through voluntary work of any kind? Are you involved with a church or other religious institution? Are you involved with any neighbourhood schemes or local politics or do you participate in any community activities, such as a local drama group, football team, aerobics class? Have you ceased to participate in regular activities because of a particular changed circumstance, such as a newborn baby or a disability or chronic illness? Have you withdrawn from activities because of loss of interest since your depression?

Are you comfortable with your status in society?

For instance, do you feel good about the way you see yourself and the way you think you are seen by other people? Do you feel suitably rewarded/appreciated for what you do? Do you feel you should have achieved more, or that others have done better than you? Do you feel you fit in? Do you feel inferior or hostile to others or often jealous of them? Do you yearn for what you haven't got?

Do you have a sense of competence and achievement?

For instance, on balance, are you doing what you want to do with your life or have your interests developed in a different direction? Do you enjoy the way you spend your time and feel satisfyingly stretched by it, or do you feel out of your depth? Do you feel unsatisfied, not challenged, stuck or bored, perhaps because there is nothing further you can achieve at work or your children have grown up and left home?

Do you have a sense of autonomy and control?

For instance, do you have sufficient responsibility in your work life or too little or too much? Can you take the responsibility for important decisions in your life? Does someone in your life have too much influence or power over you? Have you recently lost your sense of control, perhaps because of unexpected illness or the arrival of a new person at work or the introduction into your life of difficult in-laws? Do you feel you should be able to control things that, in fact, you can't control – such as how well your children do in exams – and berate yourself if things don't go as you think they should?

How healthily are your attention needs being met?

We all need to receive and give attention. But attention is a form of nutrition and, like food, we need the right kind, in the right amount, at the right time. Do you spend too much time alone? Do you feel too shy to put yourself forward or that your presence at certain occasions is of little consequence to others? Do you spend much time with an overpowering individual, who seems to seize the limelight and sap your energy in the process? Do you engage in certain activities just to win attention – for instance, turning to politics or 'spiritual' activities, just because the new love of your life is a devotee? How much sincere attention do you give to other people? Are you interested in what others think and do, or just in how their opinions and actions affect you? Do you get attention by being depressed?

Are you being 'stretched' by how you live or the work you do?

Our sense of meaning and purpose comes from making an effort to do things. So, do you have activities that interest and continue to challenge you? Are you still learning? Are you developing new skills? (Even if you are retired from work, retirement from life is not an option: you need to stretch yourself mentally and physically and set realistic goals for yourself, whatever age you are.) Do you put yourself out for other people who need you? Do you have an overarching philosophy or approach to life that helps you see life as intrinsically meaningful? Do you have a commitment to something bigger than yourself: a cause, a sport, a religion, a school, a community activity or political movement? Remember, life offers back little meaning to lazy people. Meaning comes from being stretched and engaged with the world.

It is not as complicated as you might think

Sometimes depression has an unexpectedly straightforward explanation, and it isn't the one you might expect. This is because the emotional arousal caused by so much miserable worrying prevents you from seeing what is often obvious to other people.

Rick's story

Joe once worked with a young man called Rick who had been depressed for many years and eventually ended up off work for several months because of depression. He had undergone six sessions of earlier counselling in which the counsellor had encouraged him to explore his past and, as a result, he had realised that his depression started at secondary school. Being a shy and sensitive lad, it had been an enormous culture shock for him to transfer to a large, all-boys' secondary school where one had to be confident and preferably sporty to win respect.

Of course, simply realising this didn't help Rick to deal with his depression. He remained unable to get out of bed in the mornings and spent most of his time alone, having stopped spending time with friends. He felt too humiliated to return to work, fearing all his colleagues would know why he had been away so long, and was unable to bring himself even to phone his boss. In his first session of human givens therapy, however, it quickly emerged that he felt unconfident in social situations generally, because of his experiences of being humiliated by teachers and bullies at school, and that this had had the effect of gradually closing down his life. All he really needed was to learn how to handle such situations. In that first session of therapy, Rick learned how to relax and was taught a number of social skills, which he was able to apply with beneficial effect. This boosted his confidence further and quickly lifted him out of a depression that had driven him to attempt suicide.

The millionaire's story

In another instance, a man who seemed to have everything came to Joe for help. He was a millionaire, running his own business; he adored his wife and had good relationships with his grown-up children. However, he tended towards black-and-white thinking. Because he, too, was a shy man, despite his business success, he often had to have a drink to give him more confidence at social occasions. Once, on the annual staff outing, after he had had a few drinks, he danced a little too closely, for his wife's liking, with one of the female members of staff. When his wife mentioned it, in a slightly miffed way, he over-reacted, in true black-and-white thinking style, and said, "If you feel that way, I'll never drink again!" And, true to his word, he had not had a drink since. However, as a result, he was less comfortable about attending social occasions, and soon started to refuse invitations. In a short time, therefore, his wife was refusing them too. As they ceased to go out and enjoy joint activities, their relationship started to be less satisfying – although he still loved her dearly. Because of his decision never to take another drink, he had unintentionally paved the way towards cutting off his own and his wife's social life, and their wider involvement in the community. An important need was no longer met. Their own closeness also lessened.

In addition, the businessman was fed up with working in his successful company because he no longer felt challenged by it. His business no longer stretched him and he really wanted to start another one. But, in a black-and-white way, he had assumed that his first business had to close down before he could start again doing what he really liked – building up a business from scratch. This made him feel trapped because he didn't want to close his company down and throw a loyal workforce out of work. In therapy he was helped to see that, to achieve his desire to build up a new, completely different business, he didn't actually have to close the first one down at all. He was also encouraged to take a social drink again whilst setting up a second business, and his depression became history.

Engaging with life

If you are tempted to think, "It won't be anything that simple for me," remember the negative power of black-and-white thinking. Take a look. The bottom line might be that you are no longer happy in your job or your career or your marriage, and you have been hiding this fact from yourself. That can be a frightening realisation or a liberating one. Either way, you don't have to take hasty action. Just identify what is not working and what you can do in the present to make your life work better. *For instance, we have never come across a depressed person who hadn't progressively disengaged from life – or who had ever realised that this was worsening their depression!*

> 66 **Remember the negative power of black-and-white thinking.** 99

The scenario goes like this. You feel miserable. When a friend rings up to arrange your weekly walk or a visit to the cinema, you say, "I don't feel like it this week." You don't feel much like going to your art class or the gym or bingo, or whatever it is, either, so you give that a miss too. You miss the next week and the next, and then you say to yourself that it isn't worth going back any more, as you have missed so much. Meanwhile, the friend has stopped ringing, because you've told him or her that you'll get in touch when you feel better. Without your even noticing, your social world has started to contract around you. So, when setting your goals, as we are going to discuss next, *re-engaging* with life is going to play an important part.

Set your goals

When you have realised what it is that is missing in your life, it will be easier to identify what you need to start or stop doing, to get important needs met. Set yourself some clear goals to work towards, ones that will put pleasure back into your life, and decide on the strategies you will use to achieve them.

● *Goals must be small and achievable*

Watch out for all-or-nothing depressive thinking that urges you to think too big. Make sure you start with small steps. Succeeding in those will motivate you to take larger ones. So, if you take no exercise (and we'll be discussing why exercise is so good for helping beat depression a little later), it is better to start by enjoying a short walk every evening than to determine to go to a gym and pump iron every morning and afternoon. If your self-esteem is low, it is not a good idea to decide to boost it by aiming to give up smoking and drinking, lose weight and train for a marathon, all at the same time. You are dooming yourself to failure by over-extending yourself and your self-esteem will then sink even further. Perhaps you need to feel more appreciated by others and to feel better about yourself, so one possibility might be to take on some charity work that involves you in helping others.

● *Goals must be concrete*

It is no good deciding that you want to 'be happier' or 'less of a burden on others'. That's too vague. You have to clearly define your objective. What does being happier or less of a burden look like? Unpack what it means to you. If you can't answer the question easily, try putting it this way. "If I woke up in the morning and found that I was no longer depressed, what (realistically) would be happening that is different from the way it is now?" One man who had become deeply depressed after a back injury enforced his early retirement from work said, "Well, I'd be getting out of bed in time to have breakfast with the children before they go to school. And I would talk to my wife about her day, like I used to. Even though I can't work long hours any more because of my back, I would be doing something practical in the house and the garden, to make my contribution."

Seeing this picture of his life enabled him to decide on three goals: he would set his alarm clock each morning and, regard-less of how poorly he had slept, get up to have breakfast with his children; he would ask his wife at least three questions during the day about what she planned to do/had done with her day; and he would decide on some DIY task that needed doing in the house, and do it. (This gave him even more to discuss with his wife and required him to go out to buy materials.) Of course, all of these activities started to increase his engagement with ordinary life once more and helped him regain a sense of meaning and purpose (whereas before he had been mired in self-pity, resulting in withdrawal from family and friends). When attention is directed outward into activity, there is less time to worry and ruminate, so his sleep quickly improved and his mood lifted significantly.

● *Goals must be positive*

It is no use deciding that what you need to do is concentrate on not worrying. You can't concentrate on *not* doing something. If all you are doing is thinking, "I'm worrying again! I must concentrate on not worrying. I must stop those thoughts coming into my head," you are still worrying. Turn your goal into a positive form. To stop yourself worrying endlessly, you need to find activities with which to distract yourself, so that you are too absorbed and busy to worry.

● *Goals must be focused on fulfilling the unmet needs you have identified in your life*

All depressed people gradually disengage from life, doing less and less of what they used to enjoy before, so one of your definite goals should be to reverse this, by re-introducing an activity that involves being with other people. It could be something you used to enjoy doing before or something entirely new. If you used to enjoy good relationships with people in the past, you will be able to build on those same resources to do so again. Like riding a bicycle, even if you haven't done it for years, you haven't really lost the knack. (If, however, you have always found it hard to form attachments with others, you may benefit from working with a therapist to develop the social skills that perhaps, for whatever reason, you never had the chance to learn when you were younger. These can be learned at any age, even by the very shy, and be continually improved with practice.)

Consider whether any of these ideas for re-engaging with life and experiencing pleasure is appropriate for you:

- call a friend whom you have been meaning to call for ages and suggest you get together
- go out for a walk or a meal with your partner
- take your children to the park, and join in their games
- invite a friend, or a couple of friends, for a meal at your house
- take up an activity again that you used to enjoy, such as tennis, swimming, painting, listening to live music, dancing, gardening, amateur dramatics
- walk the dog with a neighbour or go along when the neighbour takes their dog
- suggest a social drink after work with colleagues
- go to the cinema or theatre with a friend or partner

– book a holiday where you will meet new people and explore new places

– decide on a charity you would like to help and make sure this involves your being in direct contact with people – for instance, visiting at an old people's home, helping disabled children, serving hot food at a soup kitchen for homeless people

– join an evening class or go on an activity weekend, where you can meet new people.

Decide on one or two of these sorts of strategies, to start with. They should help you meet your needs for emotional and social connection. Make sure you are doing something that benefits others as well as yourself.

Other unmet needs may require you to take a deeper look at your life and explore or plan carefully for change. List your options if you are no longer happy with work or a relationship and discuss them with someone whose opinion you trust. Perhaps an appropriate strategy might be to research alternative areas of employment or look into the practicalities of mending or ending a problematic relationship. What would restore meaning and purpose to your life?

● *Goals must be appropriate*

Certain things that happen in life will not be possible to change. We cannot bring back the leg that has been amputated, or the partner who has left to live with another lover, or the husband or wife who has died. And if we are old we cannot bring back our youth. We must look at our new circumstances and set goals based on those – to regain as much fitness as possible and to take up different challenges, to engage in social activities or to meet new people to spend time with. And we can be young at heart whatever our age.

Sometimes depression occurs because someone feels stuck between a rock and a hard place, or because they have a difficult decision to make and they don't know what to do for the best. Feeling incapable of taking a decision, they slump into depression instead. But sometimes the right thing to do is *not* to take a life-changing decision, if the courses of action on offer seem as perilous as each other and there is no way of knowing at the time which one would be best. At such times, you may need to wait for other factors to click into place before your path becomes clear to you. In the meantime, it is best to concentrate on doing whatever averts unhelpful depressive thinking – for instance being active, keeping your mind productively busy, spending time with friends and eating properly. Remember, life events change all the time and the vast majority of depressed people, even left untreated, come out of it spontaneously in 4–10 months.

Scale how you feel

This is a very useful technique for providing yourself with a clear picture of how your efforts are improving your mood. On a scale of 1 to 10, where 1 is the lowest of the low and 10 is excellent, decide how you feel now. Get yourself a small notebook and draw a scale at the top of the first page, and put the date and time on it. Perhaps you think you feel dreadful and are right down at, or near, the bottom of the scale. Perhaps this is one of your better moments, because you are able to be reading this book, and so are up a little higher. (If this is the case, also scale yourself at a time when you usually feel your worst – perhaps first thing in the morning. This will give you your baseline. And you already know that you can rise up from it, because you've already got a better score in your notebook!)

Carry your notebook with you and every time you undertake an activity connected with your goals, such as going for a walk, playing a game of tennis or cooking a meal for friends, scale yourself *immediately* afterwards, noting the date and time, and the activity. Do not wait until you get home. People feel a boost in their mood after taking exercise or having a nice time with friends but later the all-or-nothing depressive thinking creeps back in and leads them to forget how good they felt, as they let themselves sink down into the doldrums again. So mark your scale with exactly how you feel when you come off the football pitch, or out of the swimming pool, or make your way home from a shopping trip or a visit to the cinema. Perhaps it is a 5 or a 6 or even a 7. That shows that you are capable of having a nice time and enjoying it. Perhaps, it is only a 2, up from 1. This may not seem much from a depressive outlook but remember it is a 100 per cent increase on how your mood was before! Next week, it might double to 4.

As you become more accustomed to getting out and about, and look forward to it, you can expect your mood to rise further and further up the scale. And if it slips back, don't worry, it's not the end of the world. In fact, it can be very useful. Think for a moment: what happened to set you back? How can you make sure that it doesn't happen again?

Another good idea is to scale yourself at set points throughout the day, and to become aware of what it is that makes your mood go up or down. Was it the phone call during which your mother criticised you that sent your mood crashing, and started you thinking about how useless and worthless you must be? Or was it the welcome phone call from a friend that sent your mood soaring and encouraged you to get on with something you wanted to do? What kinds of things seem to sap your energy and set you back and what

> **66** ... become aware of what it is that makes your mood go up or down. **99**

kinds of things boost it? This is valuable information gathering that you can use to take charge of your moods.

Separate yourself from the problem

When you are depressed, you probably feel as if you are taken over by some indescribable, overwhelming gloom. It is as if you and it are merged into one great mass of misery. But you are *not* your depression. You did not come into the world depressed as a baby. It is correct that depression is something that can overwhelm you, bring you down, even take you over; but it is something entirely outside of yourself, and it is very helpful to think of it that way.

Depression is a mindset, a misuse of your imagination (as we shall explain). It is a black cloak that can descend in seconds and last for hours. You may think of it as something that lasts for days or weeks or months or years – "I've been depressed for 12 years" people say – but when you examine what is really going on, you will remember that, hidden in those weeks or months or years are many times when the depression lifted and you felt relatively happy. And then the cloud of depression descended again. (It may be hard, at first, to remember those good times because, as we explained, the more time you spend in depression, the more familiar and practised at it your brain becomes. So, you can pull forth the miserable memories easily but find it difficult to remember the fun, laughter, delight and tears of joy.)

If you read that last paragraph again, you might spot something significant. We speak of depression as if it were a separate entity – a cloak or a cloud. You don't think of yourself as a cloak or a cloud and neither are you depression. Depression lifts and descends for a *reason*. Look at your depression as something outside of yourself and be curious to know what made it come or go or why it is still there.

> **" Depression lifts and descends for a *reason*. "**

When you do this, you are accessing your 'observing self', the rational, analytical part of your brain, instead of the primitive emotional brain we described before.

You'll find that stressful events, sudden setbacks or uncertainties (coupled with black-and-white thinking, brought on by strong emotions, and withdrawal from the enjoyments of life) that stop you getting your needs met are always at the root of depression. **The power lies not with it, but with YOU** – to let it descend or to make it lift and to recognise the signs that will enable you to send it away altogether. That is why we talk not of helping you to stop being depressed but of lifting the depression.

Remind yourself of your resources

This is a powerful technique that all effective therapists will apply, and you can do it for yourself or for someone you care for. We are not referring here to pie-in-the-sky positive thinking or making affirmations, such as "I am a wonderful person". Resources are based in reality. They are not dreams and fantasies you have but actual skills you have already demonstrated. Reminding yourself of your resources means reminding yourself not only of your talents and abilities but also of things you have successfully done in the past, which you may take for granted now, or neglect, but which actually serve as resources to draw on in the future.

For instance, having had a long-term relationship of any kind tells you that you are capable of forming and maintaining relationships (even if depressive thinking is screaming at you that you will never have another relationship again). Having had a caring relationship with anyone – for instance with your children, parents or as a professional carer – shows that you have the ability to connect with people, can put others first and can do so again. (As we have explained, depression makes people selfish. Previous instances of 'caring' proves that this hasn't always been the case and need not be so in the future.) Any job you have held, any home that you have maintained tells you something about yourself and the talents you had to deploy to perform and keep that job or run that home. If you have achieved educational or vocational qualifications or have learned a skill such as piano-playing or craftwork, or passed a driving test, that shows you have the dedication and perseverance to achieve a goal. These are all important resources.

Even what you perceive as negative qualities can be resources, if you use them positively. For instance, if you have a tendency to check things a little compulsively and make lists, direct this tendency towards scaling your level of depression and noticing what events or thoughts and feelings affect it.

When you are in a relationship that is in difficulty, bitter feelings that are at the fore may make it hard to remember that there were ever any good times between you. If you both hope to save the relationship, take the time to relax and recall the things you initially were attracted to in each other and the activities you enjoyed doing together at the start. This is a means of drawing on a powerful resource – your shared, positive experiences in your relationship history.

List all the resources you can think of, however great or small. Be creative with your interpretations of what past experiences or skills demonstrate about your positive traits and abilities to meet your needs. This will provide a firm ground for building up your confidence.

Stop the worrying

Although we are now way down the list, you need to start working at this one from the very start. Always remember that today's worry is tomorrow's depression. Stopping the worrying and ruminating will have a swift beneficial effect in the form of better sleep and more energy in the mornings. Knowing that you will feel so much better in just a couple of days or by the end of one week is highly motivating.

> " Challenge the negative thoughts that run ... through your head. "

When you experience this improvement for yourself, it will motivate you more and more to beat depression.

So this is where you must work to let the rational side of your brain get more of a look in. Challenge the negative thoughts that run, largely without your awareness, through your head. Make a conscious effort to tune in and hear what you are saying to yourself, and question it. For instance:

"I always do this wrong."
"I've done this wrong today but I did it correctly last time. It won't take long to put right."

"Mike/Mary is better than me at everything."
"Mike/Mary beat me at golf today."

"It's my fault that our marriage has failed."

"We've both done things that led to the break up of our marriage."

"I'll never get over this."
"This is painful but it will pass, as everything does."

"I should ..."   "Why?"

"I ought ..."   "Why?"

"I have to get him/her back."
"If we can't sort this out and get back together, there will be someone else for me."

"I can't cope."
"Actually, I have sorted out most things, so I am coping."

"I'm just not good enough."
"I'm doing my best."

"Oh, this is all too much! I just can't decide."
"I'll do 7/11 breathing for a moment to calm down. Then I'll decide."

Another tip is to say "Stop!" very loudly to yourself in your head, when negative thoughts repeat themselves. Make the conscious effort to switch your mind away from the negative commentary and very deliberately put your attention on to something else.

Some people lie awake, their imagination working over-time, thinking up unreasonable or unrealistic eventualities to depress themselves with, or endlessly going over events or relationships that appear to have turned out badly, replaying over and over in their mind what they 'should' have said or done. If you do this, make a conscious effort to switch on the analytical side of your brain. Ask yourself what evidence you have for thinking such a thing could happen to you, what good it does to worry about whether it might – and list what you would gain by not worrying. When thoughts are revealed to be totally, even laughably, irrational, they very often lose their power. Alternatively, distract yourself for a while with something you like doing (such as simple puzzles or crossword puzzles) that will engage your analytical brain, breaking the endless cycle of thoughts and calming you down.

EXERCISE: Widen your perspective

Before reading the next paragraph overleaf, write down three bad things that have happened to you in the last six months, and three good things. For each, write down what (or who) you think was the cause, how much of your life you thought would be affected and how long you expected the effect to last.

Now look back at what you have written. Have you taken responsibility for the bad events but given the credit for the good events to someone, or something, else? Did you think the effects would be more pervasive or more permanent than is really the case? Have you been realistic – or were you negative in your thinking? If the latter, try the exercise again but this time deliberately take a wider perspective.

Worry time

Experiment with putting 'boundaries' around bad things that happen in your life and resolve to deal with them at an appropriate time. This would mean, for instance, not bringing an argument with your partner into work and letting it adversely affect your working day or not letting your worry about a work problem affect your behaviour at your daughter's birthday party. Be aware that, even when some things go wrong, other parts of your life carry on working – and let yourself draw strength and confidence from that.

If you are an incessant worrier, try putting boundaries around worry too. Resolve to have a 'worry half-hour' late on in the day, and make a commitment to yourself that any worries that come into your head will be pushed out again and dealt with at the specified time only. (Note them down if you worry that you'll forget them!)

Laugh!

Laughter is powerful. Not only does it give our bodies a good workout – laughter relaxes the diaphragm, works the lungs and boosts blood flow – it breaks through low mood and provides an instant feel-good feeling. Smiling is good for you too. It is said that the muscle action required for smiling even a forced smile creates a calming effect on the nervous system, so, once you start, you really do feel more like genuinely smiling!

One of the first things people in depression lose is their sense of humour. We have had clients swear to us that they haven't laughed or smiled in years or that they never find anything to laugh about (clearly black-and-white thinking and selective depressive memory operating there). We all laugh. We have probably all had occasions when we have been in tears of laughter, almost hysterical and unable to stop. How easily we forget them when in the dead grip of depression.

Ivan once worked with a woman who had had 11 years of severe depression, during which time she had attempted suicide three times and been an in-patient in a psychiatric hospital on several occasions. She only came to see Ivan because her husband had brought her and she wept and wept as, slowly and with enormous effort, she told her story. She could see no point in going on and was thinking of trying to end it all again. She looked so abject and miserable that Ivan decided to try and use humour to help jolt her out of her emotional black-and-white thinking. He asked her what sort of things made her laugh. True to form, she replied, slowly and morosely, "Nothing makes me laugh".

So Ivan asked her do an experiment: to close her eyes and let her mind go back to the last time she had tears of laughter rolling down her face. He sat back and waited. After a minute or two she began to smile. Then she started to laugh, uncontrollably, and tears of laughter ran down her cheeks. She opened her eyes and told him, in between bursts of giggles, what it was that had been so funny. The laughter broke through her emotional trance state of self-pity and misery and enabled her to think rationally, so Ivan could talk to her quite normally for a while. Together, they looked at the things she had been missing in her life, since the depression took it over, and they agreed on things she could do that would start to move her out of it. (First on the list was to arrange a holiday with her husband, as for years her 'illness' had stopped them having one.)

> **" The laughter broke through her emotional trance state of self-pity and misery. "**

Why humour shakes up our thinking

We find a joke funny because the punchline is something unexpected. We appreciate a witty remark because it propels us to make a mental leap into a different perspective. We find an event funny because something occurs that is contrary to our expectations. Anything humorous switches our mindset. Thus laughter is a powerful tool that you can make use of. (The best therapists usually get people laughing!)

EXERCISE 1:

Set yourself the task of recalling the 10 funniest things that have happened in your life and relive them as you do so. (The very act of doing this will remind you that life has not been all doom and gloom and that you have had lots of fun times.) If possible, share your funny memories with someone else. The memories might be of experiences that happened to you or that you witnessed. Often things that seemed like catastrophes at the time, such as getting off a train without your luggage or losing a ticket, are very funny when you look back on them. The memories could even be of a funny moment in a film or TV show that really, really tickled you, and that makes you chuckle if ever you think of it.

EXERCISE 2:

Set yourself the task of finding something to laugh or smile about every day – and note it down, so you can remind yourself later that it actually happened. It might even make you smile again.

EXERCISE 3:

Collect some favourite cartoons (a favourite of ours is the one of Prince Charles absentmindedly making small talk with a flower: he's bending down low, saying, "So how long have you been a tulip?"), read a funny book or get out a comic film and watch it.

Uncouple unhelpful pattern matches

When events from our past cause us distress in the present, it isn't because we haven't purged them or experienced the pain of them deeply enough. It is because we wrongly associate things that happen in the present with similar but bad ones that happened in the past, and assume unconsciously that the outcome will be the same. If, at school, you were asked to speak in front of your class mates and were humiliated by a thoughtless or cruel teacher who asked you trick questions that made you appear foolish, that embarrassment might have destroyed your confidence for speaking in public as an adult. You remain fearful of being embarrassed, although the circumstances are entirely different.

This sort of scenario is a natural consequence of the pattern-matching facility of the brain, which we explained in detail earlier. We always look to relate a new experience to an old one, so that we can make sense of it. Inevitably, there are sometimes mismatches. This cannot be avoided. But the damage this does can be undone by recognising the pattern match for what it is and consciously identifying the *differences* between the new experience and the old and highlighting for ourselves what makes them ultimately dissimilar. For pattern matching is essentially quite a crude process as the following example shows. A manager doesn't take to the red-headed woman who has applied for a job, even though she is highly qualified, clearly a team player and has a lively personality. His fellow interviewers on the panel can't understand why he is so adamant against her but he insists it is 'intuition'. He doesn't consciously make the connection between the fact that the applicant has red hair, and so does his first wife, from whom he is acrimoniously divorced.

If you find yourself sabotaging new relationships, reflect on your past relationships and see what it is that you may be pattern matching to. If you are expecting John to behave like Andy, who badly let you down, think of 50 ways in which John behaves differently. For instance, he compliments you, never loses his temper, takes you out for meals, has a loving relationship with his parents, or whatever. Consciously un-matching an inappropriate pattern can help break it.

Imagine new outcomes

When a fear of failure is at the root of depression because it stops you doing something you want to do, and thus restricts your life, you may be pattern matching to a single unpleasant experience of failure in the past. Using your imagination offers a powerful means of uncoupling that unhelpful pattern match, so that you visualise yourself succeeding where previously you have seen yourself failing. (See "Use your imaginative power" on page 131.) If, however, you are pattern matching to a traumatic experience that still intrudes into your life, in the form of flashbacks or nightmares, etc., you should see a therapist who can help you take the emotional power out of the memories, so that they cease to be traumatic (see page 164). All human givens therapists are trained to do this.

The sudden depression

Sometimes it is inappropriate pattern matching that causes the sudden downward switch into a depressed mood that so often occurs in depression. You were feeling OK, even relatively upbeat, and then suddenly the black cloud descends out of nowhere and you are thinking your negative thoughts of failure and worthlessness again. But the black cloud probably didn't come from nowhere. A powerful pattern match can be evoked unconsciously by a sudden smell or a wafting fragrance, a particular sound, a particular image. But the negative expectation this raises in you is quite inappropriate or false. So if a sudden dip in mood occurs, make the conscious effort to switch into rational, problem-solving mode and try to work out what it was that precipitated that downward swerve? What unhappy circumstance do you associate with the smell or sound or image you identify that subconsciously you have pattern matched to? What *exactly* is the negative expectation you now have? Be specific. This can give you the power to break its hold. Concentrate on reminding yourself of all that is going right in your life and that this descent into depression emanates from just a momentary mismatch in your brain. Fight it. It *will* pass.

Accentuate the (realistic) positive

We are not talking here about generating a false positivity but a realistic one. Remember that depression creates an exaggerated negativity and it is important, therefore, to make efforts to redress the balance, so that you can take a wider, and thus more optimistic, perspective on the events in your life. Therapists call this 'reframing' and it is a singularly powerful therapeutic technique. When someone is too bogged down by their depressive thinking to see anything other than the all-encompassing gloom they imagine they are in, an appropriate reframe from a perceptive therapist can sometimes shift their negativity almost instantly.

For instance, a woman in deep depression told her therapist that she saw herself as weak and cowardly because she couldn't break out of an unhealthy relationship. Among the many terrible things she told him of what had happened in her life, she explained how she had had to phone her parents in Australia to break the news that her brother was dying. The therapist responded, "I don't know if I could have found the strength and courage to do that". In so doing, he was shifting her view of herself as weak and cowardly, and also reminding her of a resource she had forgotten or never recognised she had – strength and courage.

When we learn to reframe, to see another aspect or dimension to a situation and to take a new point of view, it opens our eyes to possibilities we didn't even know existed, like an unexpected, breathtaking vista that opens out before us as we emerge from a long, dark tunnel. Even if we were convinced till that moment that the tunnel would go on forever, we can't continue to hold that view in the face of such dramatic evidence to the contrary. So it is with the reframe: it creates a powerful moment of clarity, a ray of light that enhances vision. Afterwards, it is far more difficult to hold on to a rigid viewpoint – just as when, once you have seen the funny side of some misfortune that happened to you, it never seems as bad again.

A different explanation

Although it takes others to identify such reframes for us, sometimes we can work at them for ourselves – they are, in effect, a refinement of challenging negative thoughts. So, when you think something negative about yourself or someone else, try, as an exercise, to come up with a few alternative viewpoints. The aim is not to explain away problems or to avoid taking responsibility for certain attitudes or actions but to generate thoughts that open up possibilities rather than closing them down, and that consequently help you to move forward. For instance:

"My problem is that I'm too trusting. I should never embark on a relationship again."
"It is a good thing to have an open mind and not to prejudge."

"My husband doesn't love me. He never hugs me."
"Men show emotion in different ways from women. He smiles at me a lot and clearly enjoys being with me."

"I work really hard but, although I meet my targets, my boss never praises me. I can't be good enough."

"I must be highly self-motivated to do so consistently well, with no positive feedback or encouragement from my boss. Perhaps he never compliments anyone!"

"She's always going on about what's wrong with me and our relationship."

"She might be trying to make our relationship better but just be going about it the wrong way. She might be frightened of losing me."

This too will pass

The one certainty in life is that circumstances always change. People in the grip of depression don't just see their situation as dire: they see it as dire *forever* and as ruining *everything*. You now know, however, that it is the primitive thinking style of the emotional brain that makes you jump to such irrational conclusions and stops you seeing the bigger picture. It is helpful to describe events to yourself in a way that makes them appear to be the *temporary* setbacks they really are, rather than all-encompassing or unending. That means using words and phrases that create a time limitation. Through this wonderfully simple means, you can build in expectation that things will change.

For instance, when a relationship fails, the person who is prone to depressive thinking is likely to complain, "I'll never have a relationship that works!" That is a false conclusion.

More accurate, more hopeful and therefore more empowering is the realisation, "I haven't met the right person *yet*." In the first scenario, all future relationships are written off, doomed to failure before they start; in the second, failed relationships are consigned to the past but the future is left open.

> **"** The one certainty in life is that circumstances *always* change. **"**

Similarly:

"Nothing works." / "The things I've tried *so far* haven't worked."

"I can't bear it anymore." / "I've *reached the point* where I want to make changes."

"I can't ever forgive him." / "*At the moment* I'm finding it difficult to cope with my feelings of hurt."

"I can't see a way out." / "*Up until now*, I haven't seen a way through this."

Counter negativity from others

As you can see, accentuating the positive is not a trick to browbeat the mind into thinking that things are fine when they are not; it is a means of undoing the deceptions caused by emotional thinking and creating a more realistic mindset. Because people prone to depression are so ready to pick up on and internalise negativity, it is important also that you counter negativity from others that may have an adverse impact on your self-esteem. For instance, in a moment of anger or frustration, people may come out with criticisms that often they don't really mean. "You spilled that drink! You're so stupid/clumsy/inconsiderate." "Why haven't you finished that report? You are so irresponsible/slow/longwinded." They may forget their harsh comments and move on. You may carry them with you.

Children often learn to feel badly about themselves when they are 'labelled' negatively by parents or teachers, and are

The truth about self-esteem

YOU MAY well have heard a lot of talk from psychologists and others about how important it is to have high self-esteem and how dangerous it is to have low self-esteem. But self-esteem isn't something to aim for in itself. It is a by-product of engaging with life in the right way. When you master skills, have competencies you are sure of, feel good about what you do and have friends and loved ones who matter to you, and to whom you matter, you will have self-esteem. It is often when we are engrossed in an activity that holds value for us or when we are doing something for the good of others that we feel best about ourselves.

Low self-esteem is not necessarily a consequence of doing badly in life or having a depressive outlook. It may have arisen because at an impressionable age we were conditioned by other people – parents, siblings, teachers, peers – to think that we ▶

unable to speak up for themselves. Fortunately, as an adult, you can speak up and explain the problematic circumstance in a more fitting way. "I'm sorry about the drink. I couldn't avoid spilling it" or "For a moment I took my eye off what I was doing." "The report isn't finished because not all the necessary information is available yet." Or "The report was a high priority but there was another pressing deadline I had to meet first." Whether your explanation is accepted or not is irrelevant. By standing up for yourself firmly, but without being rude, you can't help but feel better about yourself.

---

were unlovable, stupid, unwanted, unworthy rubbish, etc. Learning to challenge depressive thinking in the ways we have suggested, and re-engaging with life, are natural ways to lift your self-esteem. When you are absorbed with yourself and your failings, you don't have the psychological space to focus outwards. Conversely, when you focus outwards, the more able you are to feel good about yourself.

High self-esteem is not the opposite of low self-esteem. People who think highly of themselves tend to be selfish and unrealistic. They expect always to be admired or to have their own way, regardless of the feelings or needs of others. Psychopaths esteem themselves above all others.

Self-esteem isn't static. When we don't feel good about ourselves, it may be a signal that something isn't right in our personal life or at work – something that we need to address.

Learn to cope healthily with loss

Grieving can sometimes trigger off depression. It is important to realise that grieving is a healthy, normal response to significant emotional loss. We can grieve for a person, a job that we value very highly, a home we've become deeply attached to or a pet that we've loved. When we grieve for any significant loss, it activates a biological program in the brain, the function of which is to bring the memories connected to the loss back into mind, so that we can register that the past is past and adapt to the fact. This naturally results in a feeling of sadness, which is part of the brain's way of updating its stored files, so we don't have expectations of life continuing exactly the way it was before the loss.

However, this process can go disastrously wrong if people misuse their imaginations and start to project the sense of loss into the future and run fantasies in their mind about how awful their life will be without the lost loved person or home or job or pet. Life suddenly seems totally cruel and unfair and, by excessively indulging in these types of 'fantasies', they can generate a dreadful, low, emotional mood.

It is important to be able to distinguish normal grieving from clinical depression. One accepted guideline is that if, three months after you've lost somebody that you loved, you're still obsessing about the fact and perhaps feeling actively suicidal, this is not normal behaviour. The sort of thing that can happen when people get into a pathological grieving pattern is that they turn the bedroom of the loved one into a kind of religious shrine, or they keep the loved one's personal effects laid out the way they were on the day they were killed or died. Or perhaps they ritualistically kiss the loved one's photograph first thing every morning and last thing at night. Such behaviours prevent the recovery process, maintain grieving and lead to depression.

The way to grieve healthily is to register sad feelings when they come up, be aware that they are caused by memories going through your mind and just let them go without adding to them, or making them worse by hyping up your imagination.

> **"** The grieving process can go disastrously wrong if people misuse their imaginations. **"**

If you are stuck in such pathological grieving, there are some very important things you can do to facilitate recovery. First, gradually, in your own time, go through the normal mourning task of disposing of the loved one's personal effects, giving their clothes to charity shops, and inviting friends and relatives to choose some item to remember their dead friend or relative by. Dispose of all personal effects that are on view, so that your life can move on.

Next, while still caught in this grieving process, choose a

particular morning or afternoon one day a week for your grieving. The rest of the time, resolve to live your life as normally as possible. Many religious-minded people will choose a day that has religious significance for them. Then, at any other time during the week, when a thought of your loved one comes into your mind, say to yourself, "I'll think about that during my special grieving time" and push it out of mind. You effectively ban grieving for six and a half days a week and create a specific, special time devoted to the dead person's memory.

During the rest of the week, it is really important that you focus your mind elsewhere, and do the sorts of things that you used to do and enjoy, before the loss. Maybe you took your children or grandchildren to the park on Saturdays; maybe you helped out in a charity shop; maybe you went fishing or bowling or enjoyed shopping trips. Bring those activities back into your week and re-engage in life. Remember that, as long as we are alive, we all have a contribution to make and, by being involved in life, we can help other people, through our interactions with them and by bringing them enjoyment. It may seem unfair to you that your loved one has died while you still live, but remind yourself that you have been spared because you still have a contribution to make, and it is important to go on making that contribution. You owe it to the person you loved to do that.

Use your imaginative power

Emotionally arousing worrying, which causes depression, can be understood as a gross misuse of the imagination. As we have just explained, when people dwell on the miseries they are going to face without the partner who has left them, or the hopelessness of their ever getting another job or the loss of their freedom as a result of an accident or illness, they are misusing their imaginations to generate overpoweringly negative fantasies. But the ability to imagine evolved to play a positive and useful role. Imagination made it possible to extend our survival chances as a species, rather than remain animal-like, forever trapped in the moment. And so the very thing that we misuse to develop and perpetuate depression is one of the best tools we have available to us to use in beating it.

Our imaginations are as influential as our thoughts, if not more so, in terms of directing our outlook on life. Imagination is the ability to create and 'view' in the 'theatre' of the mind scenarios other than the one we are currently in. A boy will sit by the window in a history lesson, daydreaming about what it would have been like to be a Roman soldier, an explorer, or a Chinese emperor. A woman idly wonders, as she vacuums the floor, what her life would be like now if she had married her first sweetheart. Imagination gives us mental access to the past and future instead of, as animals do, acting in awareness

> **" Our emotional brain cannot distinguish between an imagined and a real scenario. "**

only of the present.

Imagination is a 'reality generator', in that it allows us to try things out in our minds. We learn to empathise by imagining what others might be thinking or feeling. People solve problems and come up with new inventions by imagining a new way to do a particular task. Through our imagination, we can develop a concept of the future, based on what we have experienced or learned in the past. The development of imagination marked an enormous leap forward in our evolution. So whenever we imagine a catastrophic future for ourselves, based on depressive thinking blown out of all proportion, we are misusing the achievement of millions of years of evolution!

The problem is that the part of our brain that stimulates emotions has not yet evolved to be able to distinguish between an *imagined* scenario and a *real* one that is going on in the world now. This is why we can get so worked up just thinking about something. We can become angry, sexually aroused, envious, happy or sad ... *just by using imagination.*

It is never too late to start using our very own reality generator to solve problems, or rehearse a more realistic and positive future for ourselves. Some people say, "I've got no imagination to speak of." But we are not talking of startling creative powers, the production of symphonies and novels.

We are simply talking about the power to visualise. We are *all* encouraged to visualise in many settings every day. Teachers, in effect, ask pupils to visualise when they ask, "What would happen if …?" Salesmen draw on our ability to visualise when they paint an appealing picture to encourage people to buy whatever they are selling. Politicians call on us to visualise, as they make claims for what they are going to do to improve society. Children visualise as they listen to a story. And, if you are depressed, you can be sure *you* have a vivid imagination because you are using it so effectively to conjure up a miserable future existence for yourself!

Visualising success

Effective psychotherapists and counsellors make great use of visualisation to help people access, while in a deeply relaxed state, their own resources. It is a powerful means of breaking an unhelpful, inappropriate pattern match and replacing it with a better one. For instance, if someone has a fear of exams, as a result of once feeling sick during an important exam and failing it badly, they may pattern match to this one-off bad experience every time an exam looms, instead of to all the times before, when they successfully completed their exams. In a state of relaxation, they can be helped to neutralise the overwhelming negative memory (by a simple psychological technique used to resolve traumatic experiences swiftly and safely) and then asked to bring to mind some of the preceding occasions when they undertook exams successfully.

Still deeply relaxed, they will be guided through a visualisation in which they draw on that resource from the past to see themselves in the future, waiting to enter the exam room, entering it and finding their seat, waiting for the exam to start, and then working through the exam paper, all with confidence and just the right amount of motivational anxiety.

Although rehearsing success is the best way to strengthen the chances of something happening for real, it isn't magic. Rehearsing success won't help one bit if you haven't studied for your exam beforehand. What it does do, however, is take away the disabling level of inappropriate anxiety that would otherwise make all the work that *has* been done count for nothing.

EXERCISE: Try it for yourself

When you visualise a future event for yourself, you are harnessing the power of expectation. (This is why medical placebos work and why witchdoctors can kill someone with a curse.) By creating a positive expectation for yourself, you are much strengthening the likelihood of a positive outcome. Try it for yourself. Take a time when you can relax, using one of the methods we have suggested, and use it to visualise a specific successful outcome instead of catastrophe and failure on an occasion that you will shortly be facing. For instance, if you find yourself tongue-tied in social situations, imagine yourself, smiling and calm, entering a room full of people, pleased to be there. Try out some conversational lines, as you move around the room. Concentrate on making eye contact, trying out small talk, asking questions that will get people talking about themselves. Be realistic but not negative. Tell yourself, "I can do it. And the more I do it, the easier it will become."

Do this often as a means of empowering yourself, instead of worrying about how badly an event will turn out and talking yourself out of attending. This is much more than positive thinking. Doing this regularly will create healthier patterns that your brain has a chance to match to (instead of the old negative ones) when you encounter such situations for real.

Look for solutions to problems

The human brain is designed as a problem-solving organ. With our well-developed powers to plan, organise, analyse, work things out and come to conclusions, we need the stimulation of mental challenges in order to keep our brains healthy and functioning at their best. So put this to use and turn it to your advantage.

EXERCISE: Take back control

One of our important emotional needs is to feel we have a sense of control over the way we live our lives. Even when we can't control events (such as whether we need to use a wheelchair or must move home because of a relationship breaking up), we can always exert control over our responses to them. Investigating practical solutions to problems is therefore a mood-enhancing activity in itself. Instead of worrying about what has gone wrong in the past or might go wrong at some indefinite time in the future, calm yourself down through the relaxation methods we've suggested and consider your difficulties logically. List them separately. Then, for each one, think of one or more *practical* steps you could take, to start the process of positive change.

For instance, if debt is a major concern, arrange to see a debt expert at a Citizens Advice Bureau for advice about how to negotiate or renegotiate debt payments. If caring for an elderly relative without respite is bringing you down, contact the social services department to see if respite care can be arranged, or ask about local charities that provide a similar service. If this is not possible or not sufficient, think about the people you know who might be able to help you – family, friends, neighbours – and whether a rota or a 'trading' of services might help, such as mowing someone's lawn in return for an hour off to go swimming or play pool. A majority of people, even in this age of selfishness, respond when someone needs help. They just need prompting.

EXERCISE: Learn a practical skill

Join an evening class. Take up yoga, painting, cooking or learn a new language, anything useful that gets you meeting other people and doing things that are intrinsically satisfying. Perhaps you could benefit from attending a parenting class or assertiveness training. Doing so will have the twin benefits of helping you address your difficulty and enabling you to get to know new people, meeting the important need for wider social connections. (As we know, when we are depressed we tend to withdraw from our social circle and may lose connection with it altogether.)

EXERCISE: Think laterally and think creatively

Get a large piece of paper and brainstorm with yourself or another person. Jot down every idea, however implausible at first glance. One young woman we know decided to try to overcome debilitating shyness by joining an amateur dramatic group – a seemingly paradoxical step, yet, in practice, a highly astute one. In the setting of a drama group, she felt she had 'permission' to experiment with being outgoing. It also focused her attention outward. (Shy people, like depressed people, are actually self-obsessed. They worry all the time about what people are thinking of them, which inhibits their behaviour and makes them even more introverted. Making yourself talk a lot to a variety of people can wear the shyness out, so the self-obsession falls away. People will then find you more attractive and interesting as a person.)

Don't try to solve everything at once

The old saying, 'every journey starts with a single step' is true. Large or seemingly overwhelming problems need to be broken down into manageable chunks, which you can address in stages. Just starting the process and experiencing the good feeling that comes with achievement will make it easier for you to carry on.

In the encouraging case histories that we have included in the third part of this book, you will see exactly how other people have been helped to take action to deal with all sorts of seemingly daunting problems. The important thing is to start – do something to start the process rolling, however small, and you may well be surprised at the results.

Take physical exercise

Exercise lifts the mood, and there are physiological reasons why this is so. Exercise increases blood flow to the brain and raises the levels of brain chemicals such as serotonin and dopamine. If you exercise out of doors, you gain the additional benefit of natural light, which also stimulates serotonin. Higher serotonin levels make us feel good; dopamine helps create a sense of motivation, which makes us feel good too. People who are depressed have reduced levels of serotonin, not because of some problematic chemical imbalance, but because they are thinking too many depressive 'downer' thoughts, sleeping badly, unknowingly exhausting themselves, losing all motivation and not doing very much of a physical nature at all. Levels of serotonin can shift moment by moment, according to what we think and do.

It has long been claimed by some that exercise can cure depression more effectively than antidepressants. Now scientific studies confirm that it can indeed play a big part in lifting even major depression in people who have had spells as in-patients and who haven't been helped at all by antidepressants.[20] Also, twice weekly exercise classes were shown to significantly reduce depressive symptoms in elderly people unresponsive to antidepressants – if only they could be persuaded to do it.[21]

This, of course, is the big problem of depression. When you are in its grip, the last thing you think you will be able to do is drag yourself out to do anything, and the thought of its possibly being enjoyable seems ridiculous. But, again, that is just the depression deceiving you. Understanding, as you now do, how quickly it is possible to lift your mood by switching away from exaggerated, emotional thinking should provide you with enough motivation to give it a go. If necessary, start small and take a short walk. Make a point of observing your surroundings, perhaps even set yourself a task of noticing 15 different types of flowers or trees or cars or people's coats – anything that takes your interest. Scale in a notebook how you feel immediately you arrive back at your door. Look at your rise up the scale (however fast or slow) to motivate you to go the next time.

Whatever exercise you decide to take, make sure it is enjoyable and preferably not something like lone long-distance running, during which you have plenty of time to rehearse all your worries as you pound along, and add the new one of worrying about whether you are running fast enough. We recommend walking (preferably with a friend and in a pleasant area, perhaps finishing off with a drink in a pub or a café) and sports or forms of exercise that are fun and bring you into contact with other people. The exercise then becomes another means of focusing attention away from yourself and your preoccupations, and of spending enjoyable time with others.

Eat to think and feel good

What you eat can literally change the way you think and feel. What is more, as nutrition expert Patrick Holford, founder of the Institute for Optimum Nutrition, has pointed out, having enough of the right nutrients not only improves mood in it-self but helps create the energy and motivation to make the changes needed to deal with depression.[22]

Nutritionally speaking, the factors most responsible for low or depressed mood are fluctuations in blood sugar levels, deficiencies in certain nutrients and deficiencies of an amino acid called tryptophan, which is needed for making the brain chemical serotonin. Blood sugar levels can be kept on a more even keel by avoiding excess sugar in the diet, eating small regular amounts of unprocessed foods and taking a supplement containing B vitamins and chromium. It has been found that a third of people with depression are deficient in folic acid and that taking a supplement can help. Another supplement that has been tried and tested in terms of mood improvement is tryptophan or a derivative of it known as 5-HTP. In a Japanese study, when 107 depressed patients were given 50–300 mg of 5-HTP a day, over half experienced improvement in their symptoms within a fortnight and nearly three-quarters felt significantly or completely better after four weeks.[22]

5-HTP is widely available in health food shops. The recommended amount to take for depression is 100 mg twice a day. Patrick Holford points out that some supplements also contain vitamins and minerals such as B3, B6 and folic acid which can further enhance positive effects, as these nutrients help to make 5-HTP turn into serotonin.

Patrick's suggestion for a brain-friendly diet is to eat wholegrain cereals, breads, pasta and other whole foods such as lentils, beans, nuts, seeds, fresh fruit and vegetables; eggs, preferably free-range and organic; cold-pressed seed oils; and cold-water carnivorous fish such as herring, mackerel, salmon or fresh tuna.

Omega-3 fish oils have a highly important place in everyone's diet, but probably few of us eat enough fish to take in all that we need and the oil is particularly prone to damage during cooking. These oils are especially important in depression. Japan, which has the lowest rates of depression, has the highest consumption of omega-3 fish oils. Forty per cent of the membranes of the cells in our brains are manufactured from fish oils. If there isn't enough of this oil available, the wrong type of fat has to be used, and this prevents neurotransmitters, such as serotonin, from being released efficiently. So people whose diet is low in omega-3 fish oils are much more vulnerable to depression. New mothers may be at increased risk of depression after birth, if they don't increase their fish oil intake to replenish stores used by the baby during pregnancy.*

> " A daily intake of 2–10 g of omega-3 fish oils can be a powerful help in lifting depression. "

It has been shown that a daily intake of between 2 and 10 grams of omega-3 fish oils can be a powerful help in lifting depression. Two grams is a good preventative or maintenance dose and supplements are available in liquid or capsule form. However, it is advisable to get the purest and most refined form possible. (We recommend *Eye Q*, available from Boots.)

It is important to be aware that if you take these supplements in addition to antidepressants your serotonin levels may be driven too high which can cause unpleasant side effects. Consult with your GP before taking dietary supplements if you are currently taking antidepressant medication.

---

* It is a good idea for pregnant women to make sure that they get sufficient omega-3 fish oils because these are also essential for the healthy development of the baby's brain. It is best to eat fresh fatty fish or take purified omega-3 fish oil supplements (but *not* cod liver oil because this also contains Vitamin A which is harmful if taken in excess). However, because of the dangers of contaminants in sea water, pregnant women and those likely to conceive in the future are advised by the Food Standards Agency to eat no more than two portions of fish a week.

Alcohol: the false friend

Finally, if you are depressed, you may be tempted to blot out the unbearable pain and misery with the help of alcohol. This is not a good idea. Alcohol is a seductress that doesn't deliver what you think is on offer. It is itself a depressant and therefore, after a short initial bit of pleasure, soon makes people feel worse rather than better. But the expectation of that illusory mental peace it falsely promises may keep you drinking, bringing on a heavy hangover next morning and possibly a large new dose of guilt to add to the burden of depression (to say nothing of the long-term physical and mental health risks). If you recognise that you are addicted to alcohol and need help, do something about it now.

In fact all addictions, if left untreated, will trigger depression eventually because the addictive behaviour fools the person into believing they are getting their needs met in the real world, when actually the addictive behaviour is causing their lives to become more chaotic and dysfunctional. Both the addiction and the depression then need to be treated. Relatives and friends of an addict must also ensure, to avoid succumbing to depression themselves, that they continue to get their own needs met (for emotional connection to others, attention, autonomy, security, etc.) in healthy ways and avoid the all-too-common trap of becoming the addict's "doormat".

Be sensible about stopping medication

Although some people prescribed antidepressants benefit from them, many more feel that the drugs cause them to see life through a fog or that their reactions are not normal – their mood is artificially high or volatile or, conversely, even lower than before. They don't feel 'themselves'. This is particularly likely to occur when prescribed a 'cocktail' of drugs. If medication is not helping you or if you want to set about making changes in your life without the crutch of an antidepressant, do not stop taking the drugs abruptly. Although antidepressants are technically not addictive, they do cause withdrawal effects (which drug companies like to term discontinuation effects) and these can be unpleasant, painful and even dangerous, as we described earlier.

Tell your GP that you would like a programme for gradual withdrawal from your medication. Some people are reluctant to do this, fearing their GP will attribute their new, more positive attitude to the effectiveness of the drug and thus not want them to discontinue taking it. It is your right, however, to persist in what you want, and you may feel, after reading in the first part of this book about the unwanted effects of such drugs, that you particularly wish to withdraw from them. Certainly, you cannot get yourself fully well until you have stopped taking them.

Often, human givens therapists contact a GP on a client's behalf (with the client's permission), to ask for the GP's assistance in establishing a withdrawal programme while the client is supported in therapy. We have not heard of any case in which a GP has refused to agree. Most will be keen for you to regain full health by whatever means best motivate you.

Know when you can permit a brief low spell

We all have times when we go through a period when life isn't all that rosy. Life feels stressful and things get out of balance. This can easily result in our waking up with less energy on a particular day and, temporarily, we feel down and depressed and 'out of sorts'. The important thing to recognise at such a time is that this is, indeed, *temporary*. Sometimes, when this happens, you may choose to give the depression permission to be there – *but only if you put a time limit on it*. You may say, "OK, I'll let this depressed feeling be here just for a while, maybe let it run its course for the rest of the day, but I will remember that THIS TOO WILL PASS. It is a temporary state." If, on the whole, your needs are being met in your life, what usually happens is that, within the next few hours, and certainly within the next 24 hours, events will change. The phone rings; an invitation arrives; there's an interesting challenge at work. This will shift you out of the depression without your having to make a conscious effort to do it.

If you don't shift out of it, then you must take the necessary steps to make sure you do: go for a walk; get active; phone a friend, meet people etc. You don't always necessarily have to fight depression, providing you recognise that it is time limited and that you have strategies in place to deal with it if it is not gone by tomorrow.

Be ready to handle relapse

Don't be surprised if, even if you are getting on swimmingly with your new positive approach, and recovering your old enjoyment of life, you suddenly find yourself deeply down in the dumps for no apparent reason. When you have been depressed for a considerable time, your nervous system has been hyperactive for a considerable time too, and it can take a little while to settle down and stop its hair-trigger responses to minor stresses. Thus a negative thought pops into your head and overpowers you more easily than you might have expected it to. For instance, a relative asks unexpectedly to stay for the weekend, causing you to pattern match to a previous difficult visit, and you go into a slump, convinced you cannot cope.

Whenever this happens, take immediate steps to get yourself up again. Do some 7/11 breathing to calm yourself down, so that you can make use of the rational part of your brain, and investigate what it was that sent you into a downward spiral. You can bet that there was a trigger and that you will be able to identify it, once you are calm. Having done so, you can get on with deciding on a more productive response to it – challenging the negative thought or deciding to make the weekend with the relative as much fun as possible and then arranging how to divide up the extra work involved so that you don't end up doing all the chores.

Be alert to warning signs

Even when your nervous system is functioning normally again, and this depressive episode is well in the past, remember that you need to remain permanently alert to any signs that you are slipping back into depression – or, in the case of those who suffer manic depression, heading towards a manic high. It is worth repeating that depression isn't a recurrent illness; life continually throws up stresses and it is reacting to those stresses unhealthily that causes depression.

Most people with manic depression have, in the manic phase, minds abuzz with ideas and thoughts that fly too fast, and a desire to stay up late and not sleep and to get involved with lots of activities, work or fun. This is a signal that something is wrong – a stressful circumstance is being experienced and not being addressed properly. (People often come to realise that they slip into mania as a means of escape, preferable at the time to facing the stress.) Maybe it is overwork for exams coupled with the break-up of a relationship; maybe it is fear of redundancy or the pressure to meet unrealistic targets. If you suffer from manic depression, this is the time to calm yourself down (difficult and undesirable as it might seem) and resist the urge to rush around, before you are seduced into the illusion of 'escaping' into mania. Instead, ensure you eat properly and sleep enough at night. Think through the situations that are causing you stress and, if you need to, get help to decide on practical ways to handle them.

> **"**... it is possible to recognise when depression is creeping up on you. You can then take evasive action. **"**

Similarly, it is possible to recognise when depression is creeping up on you. Some people experience depression as hitting them out of the blue. But, when you have learned to be attuned to the thoughts that run through your mind, you will probably realise when you are starting to think negatively, with a focus on anger, anxiety or guilt. The moment you start to lose interest in things, feel a bit empty or uneasy, don't want to see friends or participate in leisure activities, or you stay uncustomarily late in bed for no good reason, strongly suspect that you may be falling into the thrall of depression. Face up to the stress that precipitated it and, while deciding how to cope with it more effectively, ensure you keep to plans for social and leisure activities. Work to keep your mind away from the negative thoughts. No problem or difficulty, or even tragedy, is ever lessened one least little bit by depression.

PART 3

Seeking professional help

*I*T isn't always straightforward to identify for yourself what needs are lacking in your life or what resources you have to help you fulfil them. With the best will in the world, even after making some important changes on the lines we suggest, some people may still find themselves stuck and unable to move along further on their own. That is when the help of an effective psychotherapist or counsellor is invaluable. They will ask the right questions and pick up on the information that is relevant for helping you to help yourself recover. But finding an effective one is not so straightforward, either.

Amazing as it may seem, there are over 400 different schools of psychotherapy and counselling (there is no agreed meaningful distinction between these two terms), all with their own ideas of how depression and other psychological disorders should be treated. Imagine if there were that many ways to treat a physical illness! Such disparity, and so little shared common ground between the approaches to psychotherapy, mean that people in the field are themselves confused about what really works. Behavioural therapists think that helping people change their behaviour will get them out of depression. Cognitive therapists concentrate on the idea that changing the way depressed people think about things will have the effect of making them change their behaviour. Psychodynamic therapies operate from the belief that you have to dig up all past pains and insecurities and major disappointments to understand and overcome depression. Person-centred therapy (the type most commonly on offer from counsellors in GP surgeries) maintains that the solution lies hidden somewhere inside the suffering individual; all you have to do is respectfully keep listening to them talk, with a few prods in particular directions here and there, and they'll sort it all out for themselves.

Many of these different schools of therapy have got hold of a part of the truth but unfortunately they stick to that one part and hone it, to the exclusion of everything else. This tends to unbalance the work of therapists, however well-meaning, who work from within such limited models. Of course, it is good to set people tasks to help them change problem behaviours or to help people become aware of and question negative thinking, or to listen to people with empathy, but *none of these approaches is sufficient on its own.*

All the major organisations that accredit or register psycho-therapists and counsellors include on their registers practitioners who specialise in these less-than-effective therapies. So how people term themselves professionally, which organisations or trade associations they belong to or are accredited by, and how much training they have had, are not reliable guides as to how effective they are in helping people with depression – or any other form of distress for that matter. This makes it very difficult for vulnerable people seeking professional help and for GPs wishing to refer patients to someone with psychological expertise in dealing with emotional problems.

The human givens approach to psychotherapy and counselling, which we teach at MindFields College, offers a way out of this dilemma.* We have stripped out the ideological beliefs and the cult-like preciousness of so much counselling practice. The main focus is on enabling distressed people to get their needs met and make full

> 66 The main focus of human givens therapy is to help people get their needs met. 99

and effective use of their innate resources. This means we apply whatever mixture of tried and tested techniques will help best to do that, making judgements according to individual circumstances.

---

* To find a human givens therapist close to your area, call MindFields College on +44 (0)1323 811440 or visit: www.humangivens.com/register/

Effective counselling checklist

We stress that an effective counsellor or psychotherapist will:

- understand depression and how to lift you out of it

- help immediately with anxiety (fear-related) problems including trauma (post traumatic stress disorder), phobias, panic attacks and obsessional behaviour (OCD)

- be prepared to give advice if needed or asked for

- not use jargon or 'psychobabble'

- not dwell unduly on your past

- be supportive when difficult feelings emerge, but not encourage you to remain in an emotionally aroused state

- know how to assist individuals to develop social skills, so that their needs for affection, friendship, pleasure, intimacy, connection to the wider community, etc. can be better fulfilled

- know how to help people to draw on their own resources (which may prove greater than they thought)

- be considerate of the effects of counselling on the people close to the individual concerned

- induce and teach deep relaxation (to unlock your attention from what strong emotions are keeping you focused on)

- help people think about their problems in a new and more empowering way

- use a wide range of techniques

- may set tasks to be done between sessions

- take as few sessions as possible

- increase self-confidence and independence and make sure clients feel better after every consultation. (Our advice to depressed or anxious people is not to attend therapy with anyone who says that being in therapy is usually a painful process – 'no pain no gain'. This notion originally came from old schools of psychoanalysis that believed uncovering emotional upsets about past hurts and exploring them is a good thing to do. Extensive modern research shows that such practices encourage patients to introspect even more with the result that their condition worsens, though the patient frequently doesn't recognise that this is what is happening. You may have met people who have had this type of therapy for a while and noticed that they have become even more self-obsessed and have started to use psychobabble in ordinary conversation.)

This list and the information in this book should be your guide to finding an effective therapist or counsellor. Therapists who work in tune with the human givens (even if they are not familiar with the term itself) will be happy with this list and understand it. Avoid any who are not. They may make you worse.

One important consequence of the emphasis on what people can do to meet their own needs is that the therapist can work with anyone, providing the client themselves has no prejudice about who they want to work with. It doesn't make any difference whether you are young or old, from a different ethnic or religious background, or of a different sexual orientation from the therapist you see. You establish, with their help, what needs are not being met in *your* life and set your own goals. A good therapist is concerned with your world, not theirs.

A highly important tool in human givens therapy is the ability to relax clients deeply and make use of that relaxed state to introduce positive suggestions and ideas, as well as to help people use their imaginations to change their expectations of themselves and life, and to rehearse success in new skills. When you are relaxed, the right (visual, more intuitive) hemisphere of your brain is dominant, while the left hemisphere (which is more involved in language, analysis and rational thought) takes a break. It is the right hemisphere that is most directly connected with our instinctive responses and is active when we dream, and its natural way of working is through metaphor.

Metaphor is powerful, and is used a great deal in the human givens approach, either in the form of an appropriate expression (for instance, speaking of 'calm seas' to someone who loves the sea and who is in the grip of an anxiety-driven depression) or stories. Any effective therapist, like any good teacher, has the ability to tell stories well enough to capture your imagination. The imagery thus evoked resonates with the open, imaginative style of the right hemisphere of your brain (whereas the rational part of the brain might be resistant or negative to new ways of thinking). Our natural pattern-matching facility leads us unconsciously to make the link between the metaphor, or story, and our own life, and takes on board any useful analogies.

Another important thing to find out when selecting a counsellor/psychotherapist is, do they have the spare capacity at the moment to do this work? (Any therapist can 'go off' in this regard, just as a musician will have times when they can't play well.) If their own lives are in a mess, or they are overworked, self-obsessed, or easily made emotional because of pattern matching to their clients' problems, they are likely to be, at best, useless or, at worse, harmful to you. You have to try to exercise judgement about this. If you are too upset and

> " ... the creative and perceptive input of an *effective* counsellor can help speed recovery from depression. "

emotional to do so, ask a clear-headed friend, armed with the information in this book, to interview the therapist on your behalf before committing yourself to working with them.

In the following pages we show, from case histories contributed by other therapists working from the human givens approach, how the creative and perceptive input of an effective counsellor can help speed recovery from depression.

Clive's party

Clive had been suffering depression for 12 years when he first went to see Pamela. He had been for therapy before but, as it was of the type where the client is expected to start talking and the therapist mainly listens, this hadn't gotten him anywhere at all: his main problem being that he was tongue-tied. He found it extremely difficult to open up in social situations, especially if he didn't know people well. In the therapy room, he just sat silently or nodded if the therapist tried to prompt him. As a result, he had given up on therapy as a waste of time. But his boss, who was concerned about his well-being, urged him to see Pamela, knowing that she worked in a different way.

Having built rapport with Clive and got him relaxed, Pamela asked if any significant change had happened in his life 12 years ago. This is a very important question because, in most cases, it usually uncovers what triggered the depression straight away. It certainly did in Clive's case. His marriage had ended 12 years ago. He had thought of himself as very happily married and adored his wife, with whom he did everything. They had three children, Jack, Richard and Charlotte, now in their early to late teens. Then suddenly, inexplicably as far as he was concerned, his wife left him.

His world had collapsed overnight. Because his social shyness was so severe, he had always depended on his wife to lift him out of it, enabling him to enjoy seeing friends in her company. When they parted, however, he no longer saw the friends they had shared. As he was highly nervous of meeting people socially, and of new social situations, he had, at nearly 40, become totally isolated. He then revealed that every evening he played computer games alone and drank a whole bottle of wine. Even though he still saw his children, he feared he had become wooden and boring and that they didn't enjoy the time they spent with him. Sometimes, at the weekends, he would go into crowded shopping centres, just to have the sense of life and bustle around him. "I feel I've been given a prison sentence for something I didn't do," he told her.

The only – and therefore highly important – redeeming feature in his life was his work. He was a computer salesman, and an extremely good one, happy to work long hours as it helped to fill his empty time.

Pamela asked him what he had been like before he met his wife. It soon became clear that he had always been very nervous and unsure of himself. School had been difficult for him but things took a major downturn when all the children in his class were asked to go up on the stage, one by one, and talk about themselves, as a means of auditioning for the school play. He heard other children talking confidently about themselves but, when it was his turn, he suddenly panicked, convinced no one would find what he had to say interesting. He had felt as though someone's hands were squeezing his neck and he couldn't utter a word. Eventually, humiliated, he was told to sit down. Pamela recognised that this childhood traumatic experience was still affecting his life in the present day. From his halting speech, he clearly found it difficult to talk easily or participate in conversation.

By the end of the first session, she and Clive had identified Clive's resources – for instance, he was effective at work and that showed that he had motivation and also 'stickability'. Also, he could be creative (he used to do DIY when the family was still together). They had looked at his needs (as per the list on page 80) and Clive recognised that few of them were being met. So, together, they set three goals for his therapy: to develop a social life; to make some friends and invite them round; and to develop or re-establish some hobbies.

> 66 Together they set three goals for his therapy ... 99

Pamela set him some tasks to complete before the next session: he was to write down 20 achievements, 10 personality attributes and six things he had learned through life. ("You can always learn something from the good things and the bad things that happen," she told him. "For instance, a child may scramble up a wall to see a spectacular view, while another child stays on the ground. The child on the wall falls off and scrapes his knee, which is not so good, but he has also enjoyed an experience that the other child had not dared to have.") To start countering his tendency towards negative thinking, she also suggested that he try deliberately to look for the positive aspect in things and write down three such thoughts – for instance, "It's raining, but at least that's good for the garden". Her final suggestion was that he should choose simple subjects – such as cleaning your teeth, gardening or topics in the news – and practise talking about them, as if telling someone else.

When Clive returned for his next session, he had managed to write down about 15 achievements. He had had difficulty finding good things to say about his personality, mainly reproducing the attributes that Pamela had identified as his resources the previous week. But he had put down one very significant learned life skill – that he had to be there for his children, whatever happened. (In this, he had identified something that gave meaning and purpose to his life, which was also a spur for working to improve his relationship with them.) As he had decided that he would like to take up scuba-diving for a hobby, Pamela suggested he involve the children too, and that struck him as a very good idea.

He had also recognised that, although he lived in a very friendly neighbourhood, he kept himself to himself. He had decided that his goal of making and inviting friends around would take the form of a get-together for the neighbours at his house, in a month's time. This was an adventurous target, but one he was enthusiastic about.

Pamela decided it was time to use the rewind technique (see 'How the rewind technique works' on page 164) to neut-ralise the traumatic memory of the school audition that was still getting in his way, so that it would become just an ordi-nary (if unpleasant) memory and not an emotionally arous-ing, traumatic one. Before they started, Clive scaled at 8 the level of fear that the incident aroused in him (on a scale where 1 was no fear and 10 was terror). Afterwards, he scaled it at 2. The rewind technique is carried out when a person is in a deeply relaxed state. So, while he was still deeply relaxed afterwards, Pamela built up his confidence, using metaphors such as free-flowing streams for free-flowing words. She also made much of his ability to sell, highlighting how he spoke easily in such situations and getting him to imagine doing this in social situations too.

Over the remaining few sessions, Clive's confidence rose in leaps and bounds. He kept adding to his achievements, personality attributes and positives lists, without even being asked. Pamela encouraged him to engage in a practical talking exercise; making use of the fact that he was a highly competent salesman, she asked him to 'sell' to her, in turn, a particular wine, an imagined hotel and the benefits she could derive from listening to music. (Clive had wanted to develop an interest in music but had been put off by his own lack of knowledge. Pamela used the occasion to reinforce the fact that people don't have to be experts to be interested. Indeed, it is a useful conversational aid to be able to say, "I've never heard of that composer. Can you tell me about him? What makes you like him so?")

As he had so enjoyed and benefited from the deep relaxation, she relaxed him again and asked him to visualise the bottle of wine he had been 'selling' – its appearance, the feel of the bottle, the sound of wine being poured into a glass, etc – and the same for the hotel. In this way she was helping him to be fully present and focused on what he talked about, and thus more animated and interesting – simple skills, simply taught.

His task at the end of one session was to phone three people (not connected with work) whom he hadn't spoken to in a while. At the next session, he told Pamela that he had tried to contact an old school friend. He had ended up having to contact a number of people in order to track him down and eventually reached him in Australia (quite a task for some-

How the rewind technique works

THE REWIND technique should be carried out by an experienced practitioner. It is performed when you are in a state of deep relaxation. Once relaxed, you are asked to recall or imagine a place where you feel totally safe and at ease. Your relaxed state is then deepened. You are then asked to imagine that, in your special place, you have a TV set and a video player with a remote control facility. Next, you are asked to float to one side of yourself, out of your body, and watch yourself watching the screen, without actually seeing the picture. (This is a means of creating significant emotional distance.)

You next watch yourself watching a 'film' of the traumatic event. The film begins at a point before the trauma occurred and ends at a point at which the trauma is over and you feel safe again. In your imagination, you then float back into your body and imagine pressing the video rewind button, so that you see yourself very quickly going backwards through the trauma, from safe point to safe point. Then you watch the same images, but going forwards very quickly, as if pressing the fast-forward button.

All this is repeated back and forth, at whatever speed you feel comfortable with, and as many times as you need, till the scenes evoke no emotion. If the feared circumstance is one that you will confront again in the future – for instance, driving a car or using a lift – you are asked to imagine a scenario in which you are feeling confident and relaxed while doing so. After this, the work of the rewind technique is complete. ▶

one previously tongue-tied). The school friend had been impressed by his persistence and pleased by the contact – Clive was elated.

In another session of deep relaxation, Pamela made use of Clive's knowledge of computers by offering him the metaphor that he needed to 'reprogram' his brain with the new information necessary to enable it to carry out the new tasks he wanted it to do. She encouraged him to visualise himself comfortably sitting and chatting with people, initiating conversations and so on. Clive was extremely anxious about the intended get-together with the neighbours but he decided that, before the next session, he would make invitations on the computer and deliver them. Pamela suggested he invite his children to the party too. The next week, he told her that he had not only made the invitations but had knocked at each door and handed them over personally. Ten people were due

---

Besides being safe, quick and painless, the technique has the advantage of being non-voyeuristic. Intimate details do not have to be made public. It is you who watches the 'film', not the counsellor.

A full explanation of why this technique works so well, and how to do it, can be found in our book, Human Givens: A new approach to emotional health and clear thinking. *It offers by far the best way to deal with phobic behaviour and severe trauma symptoms such as post traumatic stress disorder (PTSD).*

to attend – a mixture of couples, families with children and older people who lived alone.

When she had relaxed him, Pamela encouraged him to visualise success on the day – seeing himself collecting his children from school, enjoying working with them to prepare snacks, then warmly greeting his guests, confidently offering around drinks and making conversation. It was the last of their six therapy sessions. He rang her afterwards to tell her the party had been a complete success; that he had booked up for an evening class in Spanish conversation (to build on his school Spanish) and that he was taking his children on a scuba-diving holiday at Easter. He was also considering joining a dating agency. This man, who had previously been living a hopeless, joyless life, sustained only by his work, was now confident of his relationship with his children and of moving forward again in his life.

Nina was suicidal

Twenty-six-year-old Nina sought help after a period as an in-patient in a psychiatric hospital and several suicide attempts. She was helped to turn her life around completely in just three sessions.

Nina is Russian, and had come to Britain with her family 10 years earlier. She recalls her difficulties beginning when she was 10 – her sister had developed highly unstable diabetes, which put a strain on the whole family. One night, after an enjoyable day, her sister had a near-fatal fit and ended up in a coma for a week. Nina kept reliving the screams of pain she had heard and felt guilty at any time in the future when she enjoyed herself, fearing that this would bring on disaster again. Her mother was untrusting of other people and she absorbed that attitude and kept herself apart from others. As a result, she was a lonely child, unable to make friends easily. But she enjoyed studying and put all of her considerable energy into that.

When she arrived in England, she was sent to a boarding school to learn English (of which she spoke not a word) and to do A-levels at the same time. This was a challenge she relished, working well into the night to learn English vocabulary. But, sadly, her better understanding of the language made her realise that she was being teased by her schoolmates. They shunned her and said she had fat legs. She soon developed anorexia and also stopped enjoying her studies, although she topped the class in all of her A-levels and won a university place. She became a perfectionist and obsessive: second best would never do. Her parents had no time for her misery, telling her how lucky she was, compared with her poor sister, who by that time had gone blind and needed dialysis for kidney problems.

Although Nina excelled at university, overcame her anorexia herself and met and married her husband, whom she adored, a further bad episode in her sister's life prompted a decline in her own mental health. She sought counselling. This counselling, which required her to talk endlessly about her past, led her to make her first suicide attempt. She was put on an antidepressant and continued seeing her counsellor – in fact, was obsessed with seeing her. She made another suicide attempt and was taken into a psychiatric hospital, desperate for help, but didn't receive it. It was there that she read in a magazine about the human givens approach to depression and got in touch with Mike, a therapist in her area. At the time she met him, she was "often to be found sitting on the floor, crying and feeling suicidal, just because I was struggling to warm up a takeaway meal or there was a lot of washing to be done".

In the first session, Mike explained the cycle of depression. He also taught Nina relaxation techniques and strategies to prevent introspective, negative thoughts, so that her highly disturbed sleep pattern could be improved. He encouraged her to look to what the future might hold (rather than the past) and focused on what was uppermost in her mind at the time – her indecision/uncertainty about her professional future. She was part way through an MA and was starting to question its usefulness.

He set her a number of tasks. He suggested that she and her husband should talk together and list the pros and cons of continuing the MA. She was to do two 10-minute sessions of deep breathing each day. She and her husband were to take a daily walk, and talk about their future goals and aspirations, and they were also to look into other social activities they could take up together. (The idea was to get the couple involved in joint activities, and talking enjoyably, again, as all that had ground to a halt when Nina had been in depression.) As Nina was very studious and did little in the way of exercise, Mike also asked her to develop a fitness programme for herself.

He relaxed her deeply and reminded her of her considerable resources (she had learned English from scratch, yet beaten all her classmates at her A-levels, and had overcome anorexia on her own).

> At the second session, Nina reported that she had regained her optimism and energy within days of the first one.

At the second session, Nina reported that she had regained her optimism and energy within days of the first one. She had decided not to continue with the MA, which was a huge relief to her, and was helped to see that, although she might wish she could change circumstances for her sister, the most valuable things that she personally could contribute were humour and the chance for laughter – which her sister had appreciated and needed.

By being helped to access her rational mind, or 'observing self', while in a relaxed state, Nina was able to realise for the first time that, by telling herself to concentrate on not thinking about suicide, she was actually *making* herself think about it – the 'don't think of a pink elephant' type of impossibility. This was a major revelation to her and stopped her nagging thoughts about suicide, literally overnight.

In her final session, Nina reported two months of "very positive mental health and energy" but also that just lately she had started to slip back, she wasn't feeling so good or energetic anymore. The reason soon became clear. Nina was expecting to be offered a high-powered job as a financial analyst and was also hoping to be accepted for a fast-track Civil Service career, but she was 'in limbo' whilst awaiting an outcome. Mike had recognised that she was happiest and most energetic when busy and mentally stretched and that it was when she was bored that she tended to relapse into negative introspection. He also felt she needed to address her inability to contemplate – and therefore handle – failure and so, to address her 'all-or-nothing' mindset, he set her the task of researching other career options. This also kept her mind busy and focused outwards. He suggested she might consider taking a job as a waitress, while she was awaiting career offers – as a way of increasing the time she spent relating to other people, reducing the time available for introspection and giving her an income.

These turned out to be very helpful suggestions. Nina did not get picked for the Civil Service placement but, instead of going into depression, that very evening she was evaluating other career moves, including the job as financial analyst. She eventually accepted this challenging post – and she also decided to keep on working as a waitress part-time.

Enjoying her life again had, ironically, led to a resurfacing of the traumatic flashbacks she had experienced after her sister nearly died after an enjoyable day. The rewind technique banished these quickly and effectively.

In an email to Mike some time after her third and final session, Nina said,

"I've gradually taken myself off the antidepressant I was prescribed. Not having to rely on the 'happy pills' (which truly they are not) is a wonderful feeling on its own, but feeling how strong I actually am is even more rewarding. My sleeping pattern is now back to normal. Coming off the antidepressants has helped to reinforce all of my normal energy, enthusiasm, optimism, pride and assertiveness. My feelings now are not 'foggy' or 'inhibited' as on the tablets. I think people don't realise that antidepressants not only 'numb' the distress and sorrow; they also make it difficult to enjoy life. I am now happily looking forward to my future."

Arussa learns to look ahead

Some years ago, a 30-year-old woman called Arussa sought therapy from Pat. Arussa dated her depression from the age of 11, when her father had taken her on a skiing holiday abroad and she had seen him killed in a freak skiing accident. Not only did she have the trauma of this experience and of, initially, being alone in a foreign country to contend with, but she next had the shock of being shunned by her dead father's family. They had never approved of her parents' mixed-race marriage and were only prepared to tolerate Arussa and her mother's presence in their lives while their son was alive. Arussa's mother was extremely bitter about this and not psychologically strong enough to give Arussa the support and understanding she needed. Arussa, unsurprisingly, grew up distrustful of relationships and with a very low sense of self-esteem.

She had coped as best she could and, happily for her, had managed eventually to have a relationship with a man which lasted, largely because he was so besotted with her. But she was deeply unhappy and was easily sent into panic and depression if things didn't go well, at home or at work. She was a classroom assistant at a local primary school, having dropped out of university, failing to fulfil her true potential.

Eventually, she decided she needed help and her GP referred her to the psychiatric team at a leading teaching hospital.

They undertook to assess her, a process which took six sessions over a period of six months. After the six months, they decided she was indeed depressed and would take her on as a patient, but informed her that there was a seven-month waiting list. Having held herself together till this point, she could bear no more. Although she arrived for her session with Pat, she had in her bag the pills she planned to use for an overdose, if she didn't feel any differently afterwards.

From just talking with Arussa, straightaway Pat could see her true qualities. She had a generous heart, a natural optimism that had never been recognised or tapped into and an eagerness to learn. "It was clear she deeply wanted to move forward in her life. Helping her was largely a matter of making her aware of her innate resources, and showing her how to use them," recalls Pat.

She helped her focus on the positives already in her life (particularly her strong relationship) and what was out there, within her grasp, instead of focusing on the past. She taught her to externalise the depression, instead of seeing it as an intrinsic part of her personality, suggesting she give it a name. They settled on Lump. As a result, Arussa learned better to compartmentalise her emotions – if someone was critical of her at work and she was tempted instantly to blame herself and relive all her past inadequacies, she could recognise that Lump had pitched up on the scene and sent it away again.

Arussa's recovery took just four sessions, during which Pat used the receptive state of deep relaxation to build up Arussa's confidence further, telling her stories that, consciously or unconsciously, Arussa could relate to her own life. One that resonated particularly strongly with Arussa was the story of King Canute, who tried in vain to hold back the waves. By this means she learned that there were things she could control and things she couldn't, and it was pointless to waste time and energy agonising over anything she couldn't change – such as what had happened in her past or certain circumstances in the present. (For instance, the class teacher she worked with had a difficult personality, which made Arussa's job very difficult. She couldn't change the teacher's personality but she could decide to change her job.)

> **66** Arussa learned there were things she could control and things she couldn't. **99**

Arussa felt happy and confident enough to stop therapy after four sessions but Pat asked her to come back a couple of months later, in case in that time Arussa might have suffered a relapse. "I wanted her to realise that, even if something occurred that caught her off-balance and brought her down, it was easy to get back up again. That is exactly what happened."

Today, Arussa is an assistant headteacher, with headship

in her sights. In the intervening years, she took her degree, trained as a teacher and worked up through the ranks. She makes good use of her skills and attributes, bringing out the best in other teachers and being innovative and still ready to learn. Her relationship is even stronger and is now a partnership between equals.

Bella's new friends

A distraught mother got in touch with Pamela about her 31-year-old daughter, Bella. Thirteen years previously, Bella had been diagnosed by her GP as suffering from manic depression and had been on drugs for it ever since. She had dropped out of university and had returned to the family home, doing nothing with her life for all those years. Just recently, having been persuaded to go with her family to visit relatives abroad, she had felt so panicky that she couldn't get out of bed most mornings, and their stay had had to be cut short.

When Pamela asked Bella what had happened all those years ago to make her depressed, she said that she was shy and unhappy and felt so terrible that she had had to leave university. She had told her GP that sometimes she felt happy and sometimes she felt really sad, and he had decided, on that basis, that she suffered from manic depression and that she would need to take drugs for the rest of her life. She hated the idea and felt miserable on the drugs.

She said that, before she became depressed, she had been happy, outgoing, loved school and was good at exams. Even during her depression, she could often motivate herself for a day, then would collapse and spend two weeks in complete inertia. Pamela reframed her experience for her. She said, "Clearly you are a determined young woman who wants to live life but some important needs are not being met, and that is what brings you down." This made much better sense to Bella than a diagnosis of manic depression.

Pamela learned that 13 years ago, at university, Bella had had an experience she interpreted as bullying. It then emerged that she had been seriously bullied by a group of girls at the age of 10, when she was a new girl at a school in the area her family had just moved to. It was a highly upsetting time but, because she was outgoing and clever, she had managed to cope. At university, she fell out with some girls she had thought were her friends. One afternoon she saw them laughing and, because they glanced at her, was convinced they were laughing at her. It seemed she had pattern matched to the earlier trauma of being bullied but this time she had fallen to pieces. She didn't dare talk to other girls after that, fearing she would be made fun of. At this stage she received her diagnosis.

Pamela explained to Bella how the cycle of depression works, and how the imagination is a marvellous resource but we can sometimes unwittingly misuse it. Bella was very interested to learn about inappropriate pattern matching. She responded very well to the rewind technique, in which she re-ran the memory of both the original bullying incident and the university episode, until neither had the ability to arouse her emotionally anymore.

With the aim of helping Bella to engage with the world again, Pamela set her the task of taking up some hobbies. Bella had used to like walking, playing the piano and cooking, and said she would like to rediscover her pleasure in them. At the end of the session, she said, "I can't believe how I feel! I'm so relieved."

When she returned three weeks later, she had done some cooking and had signed up to join a cordon bleu cookery course. She had started playing the

> ❝ I can't believe how I feel now! I'm so relieved. ❞

piano and walking again, and understood how exercise helped her to feel physically good. In deep relaxation, she visualised herself feeling comfortable around women and having women friends once more. Pamela particularly directed her to 'see' on their faces not the feared mockery but pleasure in Bella's company. She gave Bella a metaphor for how easy change could be. "You can go to bed at night and the view from your window is as normal. Then you wake in the morning and the garden is covered in snow. You haven't had to do anything to make that happen, but can just enjoy it."

As Bella was keen to stop her medication, Pamela suggested she see her GP to tell him about the therapy and ask for his advice about tapering off.

Bella needed no more therapy after that. Five months later, she sent Pamela a letter, in which she said: "I have started going out again and making friends and feel as though I have begun life afresh. I've made four women friends, who are great fun to be with. Two of them I met at work – I am a part-time receptionist at the moment. I'm doing this while I decide on a career, and I am enjoying deciding what I want to do next, rather than just jumping into whatever is offered to me. I can't remember the last time I was so happy. Thank you for giving me my life back!"

As Pamela commented, "No she *took* her life back. All those words – *decide, enjoying*, jobs expected to be *offered* her – that isn't a negative, depressed person talking!"

* * * * *

Depression as a will-o'-the-wisp

We hope this book has helped you to see that it is emotionally-driven imagination generated by worrying about unmet emotional needs, which starts off the self-perpetuating cycle of depression. More importantly, we hope you see how quickly and easily depression can be defeated.

Depression is not a demon. It is not a mystery. And it is not a biological illness. When you use the techniques and approaches we suggest (with or without the help of a therapist), all depression, however severe, will soon become no more than a will-o'-the-wisp, an illusion – utterly insubstantial. Please don't allow it to take up any more of your time. Whatever stage you are at on your life's journey, focus your attention outwards and rediscover the fact that meaning, purpose and joy come from taking positive, challenging action that stretches you in the real world.

References

1. Danton, W, Antonuccio, D and DeNelsky, G (1995). Depression: psychotherapy is the best medicine. *Professional Psychology Research and Practice*, 26, 574.

2. Seligman, M E P (1991). *Learned Optimism*. Alfred Knopf. New York.

3. Department of Health *National Service Framework for Mental Health*. See: www.dh.gov.uk

4. *Medical Health Index* (1999). IMS Health.

5. Ferri, E, Bynner, J and Wadsworth, M (2003). *Changing Britain, Changing Lives: Three generations at the turn of the century.* Institute of Education, London.

6. Lane, R E (2000). *The Loss of Happiness in Market Democracies*. Yale University Press.

7. UNICEF (1993). *The Progress of Nations*. United Nations, 45.

8. *The Global Burden of Disease* (1997). World Health Organization, Geneva.

9. Nemeroff, C B (1998). The neurobiology of depression. *Scientific American*, 278, 6, 28–35.

10. Peterson, C and Seligman, M E P (1984). Causal explanations as a factor for depression: theory and evidence. *Psychological Review*, 91, 341–374.

11. Griffin, J and Tyrrell, I (2004). *Dreaming Reality: How dreaming keeps us sane, or can drive us mad.* HG Publishing, East Sussex.

12. Robertson, I (2000). *Mind Sculpture: Unleashing your brain's potential.* Bantam Books, London.

13. Teasdale, J D (1988). Cognitive vulnerability to persistent depression. *Cognition and Emotion*, 2, 247–274.

14. Glenmullen, J (2001). *Prozac Backlash*. Simon and Schuster, New York.

15. Fergusson, D, Glass, K C, Waring, D and Shapiro, S (2004). Turning a blind eye: the success of blinding reported in a random sample of randomised, placebo controlled trials. *British Medical Journal*, 328, 432–434.

16. Questioning antidepressants. *Health Which?* February 2002.

17. Helgason, T, Tómasson, H and Zoega, T (2004). Antidepressants and public health in Iceland: time series analysis of national data. *British Journal of Psychiatry*, 184, 157–162.

18. Baron-Cohen, S (2003). *The Essential Difference: Men, women and the extreme male brain*. Allen Lane, London.

19. Griffin, J and Tyrrell, I (2003). *Human Givens: A new approach to emotional health and clear thinking*. HG Publishing, East Sussex.

20. Dimeo, F, Bauer, M, Varahram, I, Proest, G and Halter, U (2001). Benefits from aerobic exercise in patients with major depression: a pilot study. *British Journal of Sports Medicine*, 35, 114–117.

21. Mather, A S, Rodriguez, C, Guthrie, M F, McHarg, A M, Reid, IC and McMurdo, M E (2002). Effects of exercise on depressive symptoms in older adults with poorly responsive depressive disorder: randomised controlled trial. *British Journal of Psychiatry*, 180, 411–415.

22. Holford, P (2003). *Optimum Nutrition for the Mind*. Piatkus Books, London.

INDEX

this too will pass 124–5, 146–7
thyroid antibodies 61
time pressure 13
traditional societies 7–9, 11
traumatic events
  case studies 166–75
  preventing needs being met 32
  rewind technique 162, 164–5
  uncoupling pattern matches 120

U

uncertainty 14
unfulfilled expectations, dreams
  35–45

V

visualisation 88–9, 131–5

W

warning signs 148–50
winter depression (SAD) 65–6
women 60–5, 69–77
work, needs audit 94–5
worry time 114
worrying 179
  postnatal depression 63–5
  REM sleep 37–40
  stopping 111–14

Human Givens:
A new approach to emotional health
and clear thinking

"A wonderfully fresh and stimulating view of dreaming, evolution, and human functioning. *Human Givens* also provides both an encompassing model and practical, specific applications to enhance the effectiveness of psychotherapy. It will deepen and widen every reader's perspective."
Arthur J. Deikman, M.D., Clinical Professor of Psychiatry, University of California

"Big idea... Key insight... Weekly excavation of your painful past in an attempt to understand your present depression has never seemed so foolish." *Financial Times*

"Important original work ... both aesthetically pleasing and of immense practical use... has great relevance to all areas of life... could save (tax payers) millions of pounds. A remarkable achievement which should attract the attention of any truly curious human being."
Dr Farouk Okhai, Consultant Psychiatrist in Psychotherapy

"*Human Givens* is the most practical and intuitive book I've read in years. People have been speculating about the utility of dreams for decades, but I think you guys have it hammered."
Charles Hayes, Autodidactic Press, USA

"Psychology doesn't have to be difficult and mystique has no part especially when the writers cross boundaries to take from all quarters and from there synthesize with such clarity. Some purists may not like it [*Human Givens*] but broken fences facilitate a wider view and allow one to see further." *Leo Kingdon*

"A quiet revolution." *New Scientist*

Human Givens: A new approach
to emotional health and clear thinking
by Joe Griffin and Ivan Tyrrell

Published in paperback by HG Publishing (2004) ISBN: 1-899398-317

Dreaming Reality:
How dreaming keeps us sane, or can drive us mad

"*Dreaming Reality* exquisitely scythes through the Gordian knot created by past dream theories. Even better, like all the very best explanations, its central theme is as far-reaching as it is intuitive. Through a fascinating combination of dream examples and scientific findings, it provides lucid and compelling evidence for how our night and daydreams not only mould our personalities but also lie at the very heart of being human." *Dr Clive Bromhall, author of 'The Eternal Child'*

"A remarkable book that makes compelling reading. Griffin and Tyrrell's adriotly written text challenges traditional views on our knowledge and understanding of the mystifying covert world of dreams." *Professor Tony Charlton, Professor of behavioural studies, University of Gloucestershire*

"This book is revolutionary in more than one way. Past and sometimes overlooked research is re-evaluated, and a persuasive theory emerges... long overdue to my mind." *Doris Lessing*

"For anyone who has speculated on the meaning and purpose of dreaming, Griffin and Tyrrell's astounding insights light up the dark corners of the mind. Not since 1964 when Carl Jung's book *Man and his Symbols* was published has anyone set out to write so conclusively on dreaming for a wide audience.

Griffin and Tyrrell [propose] that dreaming functions to cleanse the undischarged emotional arousals of the day and they explain how this happens through metaphorical pattern-matching. From this one sets off on the journey to understanding the true causes of (and routes to healing) depression.

This book is revolutionary in thought, revelatory in content and will be established as the most important twenty-first century milestone on the road to accessible mental health treatment for all. It's a must for all who live with mental illness or work for its relief." *Ian Hunter* OBE

Dreaming Reality: How dreaming keeps us sane, or can drive us mad is published in hardback by HG Publishing (2004) ISBN: 1-899398-368